Praise for *You Lost Me*

"The next generation is leaving institutional Christianity but they are drawn to movements of God that invest in relational discipleship. Kinnaman sounds the alarm while providing savvy advice on connecting with disaffected youth."

Leadership Journal, Top Book of 2011

"Kinnaman is unafraid to criticize in the name of reform, and he bolsters his research arguments with concrete suggestions for improvement. This practical problem-solving approach, along with his repeated assertion that 'every story matters' and his occasional touches of the personal—whether his own opinions and sympathies or excerpts from interviews—make the work a must-read for anyone concerned about the future of Christianity."

Publishers Weekly

Praise for *UnChristian*

"This is a wonderful, thoughtful book that conveys difficult truths in a spirit of humility. Every Christian should read this, and it will likely influence the church for years to come."

Publishers Weekly, starred review

"This is an engaging, challenging, and morally compelling study, and it deserves a wide readership."

Library Journal

"*unChristian* could be a milestone on the way to a changed church—one that represents Christ in humility, love, grace, and service toward all. Essential reading for all Christian leaders."

CBA Retailers

"For leadership in all areas but especially in youth and young adult ministry, it's not just a read-through but an excellent reference to keep on hand."

Christian Retailing

Praise for *Good Faith*

"A wise and accessible guide to 'being a Christian in the public square' today. For nearly a generation there have been voices calling the church to rethink its mission and life in the post-Christian West, but this volume brings those more general and academic discussions down to earth and up to date."

Tim Keller, Redeemer Presbyterian Church, New York City

"A landmark and thought-provoking read—that could become literal good faith through us to further a humble and winsome common good. A highly anticipated and needed must-read for every engaged thinker."

Ann Voskamp, author of *One Thousand Gifts* and *A Holy Experience*

"A trustworthy guide through the emerging post-Christian order that neither denies the urgent reality of the bad news nor downplays the radical hope of the Good News. This prophetic book inspired me to rethink my own assumptions about how to live faithfully in our American exile."

Rod Dreher, journalist and author
of *The Benedict Option*

"A timely reminder that Christians don't have to conform in order to survive. It encourages those of us with deep convictions not to cower but to boldly speak truth with wisdom and love. Radical followers of Jesus can be relevant."

Francis Chan, pastor, teacher, and author
of *You and Me Forever*

"Speaks prophetically to the church by diagnosing our condition and prescribing a course of powerful treatment. God's people must practice Spirit-filled faithfulness in a culture defined by allegiance to self. This book is a trustworthy guide for that practice."

Christine Caine, author and founder of A21 Campaign

"Will equip you to live in a courageous, intelligent, loving, and faithful way in our changing culture that has grown less friendly to followers of Jesus."

Derwin Gray, pastor of Transformation Church
and author of *The HD Leader*

"Calls Christians to use their faith to make society a better place, and more importantly, they equip us to walk in courage and hope. The Christian life is a counterculture journey, for it is a light shining in darkness. This is exactly what the world needs. It is impossible for light not to change darkness, unless that light is hidden."

Banning Liebscher, founding pastor of Jesus Culture

"Gives clarity to the challenges Christians face while inspiring us to recognize the power we have to rekindle a flame that will transform our world."

Richard Stearns, president of World Vision US
and author of *The Hole in Our Gospel*

Faith
for
Exiles

Faith for Exiles

5 Ways for a New Generation
to Follow Jesus in Digital Babylon

David Kinnaman
and **Mark Matlock**
with Aly Hawkins

BakerBooks
a division of Baker Publishing Group
www.BakerBooks.com

© 2019 by David Kinnaman and Mark Matlock

Published by Baker Books
a division of Baker Publishing Group
PO Box 6287, Grand Rapids, MI 49516-6287
www.bakerbooks.com

Printed in the United States of America

Library of Congress Cataloging-in-Publication Data
Names: Kinnaman, David, 1973- author. | Matlock, Mark, author.
Title: Faith for exiles : 5 ways for a new generation to follow Jesus in digital Babylon / David Kinnaman and Mark Matlock with Aly Hawkins.
Description: Grand Rapids, MI : Baker Books, [2019] | Includes bibliographical references.
Identifiers: LCCN 2018061474 | ISBN 9780801013157 (cloth)
Subjects: LCSH: Church work with young adults. | Evangelistic work. | Discipling (Christianity) | Young adults—Religious life—Statistics. | Internet—Religious aspects—Christianity. | Christianity and culture.
Classification: LCC BV4446 .K56 2019 | DDC 259/.25—dc23
LC record available at https://lccn.loc.gov/2018061474

ISBN 978-0-8010-9418-7 (ITPE)

19 20 21 22 23 24 25   7 6 5 4 3 2 1

To Jill and Jade,
whose resilient faith and love for Jesus
inspire us every day

Certainly there was an Eden on this very unhappy earth. We all long for it, and we are constantly glimpsing it: our whole nature at its best and least corrupted, its gentlest and most humane, is still soaked with the sense of "exile."

J. R. R. TOLKIEN

Contents

Start Here

Digital Babylon and Resilient Exiles

feel like there are a million things I'm forgetting to remind you," I tell my firstborn, Emily. We are three hours into a seven-hour trip to move her in for freshman year. The silver Kinnaman minivan is packed with crates of clothes and dorm room décor, and I am trying to cram in all the parenting wisdom that comes to mind. What to eat. How to manage her bank account. What to do in an emergency. How to remember what's on a guy's mind.

How much I love her.

How to stay committed to Jesus.

Most of our family attended Christian colleges. I did. My wife—Emily's mom—did too. Christian higher education shaped my parents, my siblings, and their spouses. But that option wasn't best for Emily. She graduated as valedictorian from an academically challenging high school and, as a great student with mountain-sized ambitions, had a specific science career in mind: genetic research. (She geeks out like her dad.) None of the Christian schools that felt safe and wholesome enough to me seemed prestigious or rigorous enough to her. So Emily elected to attend a state school. And not just any state school: University of California, Berkeley.

My perception of that legendary Bay Area institution? Let's just say I was dead set against Berkeley when Emily put it on her list of possibilities. I tried to ignore the possibility that it *was* a possibility. Given a series of unexpected circumstances, however, attending became a real option—not just an unthinkable one. She visited and loved it. I realized just how elite the school is, especially for young scientists. Oh, and God changed my mind. (I'll tell you later how that happened.)

So now, alongside conviction that the Lord is leading my brilliant, talented, and driven eighteen-year-old daughter to Berkeley, I also feel trepidation. On campus, Emily beams with pride as she power walks the hillside, showing us highlights she remembers from previous tours. "These are reserved parking spots for Nobel Prize winners who teach at Cal!" As she leads us through Sproul Plaza, a landmark infamous for its rowdy political protests, the fading light of a Northern California evening hangs over imposing buildings. I know Emily possesses great reserves of physical and spiritual strength, yet I can't help but wonder, *Have we given her a resilient faith that will last?*

■ ■ ■

I am not just a worried father; I have professional reasons for my concern. In my work as a social researcher, I've interviewed tens of thousands of tweens, teenagers, and young adults. Using a variety of quantitative and qualitative research methods, my company, Barna Group, examines the spiritual journeys of young people.

A lot of what we hear is distressing.

It's a concern shared by my coauthor, Mark Matlock, who has spoken to nearly a million teenagers and parents, and written dozens of books about growing mature and lasting faith. And like me, he is a father to young adults and teens.

We have each been working with and for the sake of young people and the church for more than twenty years. So we've been thinking for a while about how to grow young disciples—and, at the same time, we've been parenting young disciples.

Here is a big data point that keeps us up at night.

The 2011 book *You Lost Me* argues that the church has a dropout problem. At the time we collected data for that project, 59 percent of young adults with a Christian background told us they had dropped out of church involvement—some for an extended period of time, some for good.

In less than a decade, the proportion of eighteen- to twenty-nine-year-old dropouts has increased. Today, nearly two-thirds of all young adults who were once regular churchgoers have dropped out at one time or another (64 percent).

Our contention is that today's society is especially and insidiously faith repellent. Certainly, God's people have weathered hostile seasons in the past; church history reminds us that living faithfully has never been easy. But our research shows that resilient faith is tougher to grow today using the cultivation methods we relied on throughout the twentieth century. This leads to our central claim in *Faith for Exiles*.

> Young non-Christians are avoiding Christianity,
> and young Christians are abandoning church;
> however, by cultivating five practices, we can
> form and be formed into disciples of Jesus
> who thrive as exiles in digital Babylon.

15

Faith for Exiles is different from my previous books on faith and the next generation, which uncover how the Christian community sometimes fails to portray Christ's love so that young adults can perceive and receive it (*unChristian*, 2007) and, to young church dropouts, fails to make a case for itself (*You Lost Me*, 2011). Thanks to the research behind those projects, and dozens of other Barna studies among the next generation, we know a great deal about what is going wrong in the North American church's efforts to connect with young Christians and non-Christians.

But what, if anything, is going right?

More than a decade's worth of research with nearly one hundred thousand teens, young adults, parents, and church leaders reveals how young faith *can* mature and thrive in cultural exile. This book distills what we've learned thus far about passing on lasting faith in Jesus in a culture increasingly indifferent and sometimes hostile to Christianity.

Even now there are seeds of hope germinating in the cracks, breaking through in places such as England, Scotland, Ireland, Canada, and Australia—societies that are even more post-Christian than our own. Our research shows this is happening in North America too. And what we find confirms what Christianity's long history records: the roots of faithfulness often sink deeper in anxious, unsettled times. Faith can grow even—and sometimes especially—in the darkest of places.

Remember Jesus's parable of the sower, in which a farmer scatters seeds on various kinds of ground? It illustrates the spiritual receptivity or resistance of the human heart, reflecting a range of possible responses to the good news of God's kingdom. Through many centuries, this story has been used as a sort of growing guide to help Christians diagnose the condition of the soil they are working with and then provide suitable light, proper pruning, and beneficial care.

As in that ancient story, today the soil of many hearts is rocky, dry, and dusty, or filled with thistles and weeds, stifling what really matters. The age-old questions of being human remain unasked, shriveling like neglected seedlings. Deep spiritual longings, which ought to be lovingly tended and skillfully cultivated, are choked to death by binge television, immersive gaming, and social media scrolling. As we will say many times in the coming pages, technology and the lighted rectangles we gaze at all the time aren't bad in and of themselves. But if we are not vigilant and intentional, digital Babylon glitzes and blitzes our days so completely that we never get around to pursuing the deeper things of life.

We believe this generation wants and needs more. And we believe the abundant way of Jesus, the family of God called the church, and the ancient call of Christian mission can answer the stifled longings of this anxious age.

Welcome to Digital Babylon

Maybe you remember that ad from a few years ago in which a young adolescent boy asks, "Google, what is 'glossophobia'?" A warm female voice gently informs him, "Speech anxiety is the fear of public speaking." He clicks "explore more" on his Nexus tablet and launches audio of Franklin D. Roosevelt's first inaugural speech on the steps of the US Capitol, which soars over an inspiring video montage of Google coaching the young man's preparations to give a speech in class.

We can tell the young man's speech is a big success because his classmates burst into applause—and because an attractive

17

girl shyly smiles at him. Surprised and sheepish, he smiles back.

Jump cut to the ubiquitous Google search bar.

"How do I ask . . ." the boy types, ". . . a girl out," the drop-down bar suggests, because his trusty Google device can see into the hopeful places of his tender heart and wants to be his ever-present, all-seeing, secret-keeping BFF.

Many of us today turn to our devices to help us make sense of the world. Young people, especially, use the screens in their pockets as counselors, entertainers, instructors, even sex educators. Why build up the courage to have what will likely be an awkward conversation with a parent, pastor, or teacher when you can just ask your phone and no one else will be the wiser?

When it comes to technology, the path of least resistance is not scorn-worthy because it's easy. It's praiseworthy because it's efficient.

Google searches are wonderful benefits, mostly, of life in the modern world. Who hasn't found their life improved by access to the right information at the right time? Watch a step-by-step tutorial on repairing your dishwasher. Listen to your favorite song. Discover a new recipe. Shop for your friend's birthday gift right now, before you forget. Confirm for the foolish person disagreeing with you that the villain in the first *Die Hard* movie is, in fact, Alan Rickman (not Jeremy Irons).

The virtual possibilities are virtually endless. Screens are portals to more rabbit holes than Alice could visit in many thousands of lifetimes—and a few even lead somewhere helpful.

Yes, there's the rub: instant access to information is not wisdom. In a 1965 sermon, Dr. Martin Luther King Jr. could have been talking about our present moment when he asked,

"How much of our modern life can be summarized in that arresting dictum of the poet Thoreau, 'Improved means to an unimproved end'? . . . We have allowed our technology to outdistance our theology and for this reason we find ourselves caught up with many problems."[1]

How do we find the rabbit hole that leads to real, worthwhile wisdom for living well and following Jesus in an accelerated, complex culture?

By *accelerated*, we mean everything moves faster: the news cycles, the speed of information, the pace of life, the rate of change. This is the screen age, after all. Digital tools, devices, and content drive our perceptions and experiences of reality. They offer an illusion of total control and a mirage of complete access to the world. As Andy Crouch writes in *The Tech-Wise Family*, technology makes things *easy everywhere*.[2]

By *complex*, we refer to the fact that everyday life feels increasingly complicated and uncertain. It is difficult to predict the relationship between cause and effect, to understand what outcomes (intended and unintended) will result from a given course of action, or even to get a complete picture of all the variables involved.

You Lost Me identifies three trends shaping young adults and our culture more broadly: *access* (which, thanks to "Wi-Fi everywhere," is exponentially more amplified today), *alienation* (from institutions and traditions that give structure and meaning to our lives), and *authority* (which, like institutions and traditions, is increasingly viewed with suspicion).

In the years since that book came out, we at Barna have adopted a phrase to describe our accelerated, complex culture that is marked by phenomenal access, profound alienation, and a crisis of authority: *digital Babylon*.

Ancient Babylon was the pagan-but-spiritual, hyperstimulated, multicultural, imperial crossroads that became the unwilling home of Judean exiles, including the prophet Daniel, in the sixth century BCE. But *digital* Babylon is not a physical place. It is the pagan-but-spiritual, hyperstimulated, multicultural, imperial crossroads that is the virtual home of every person with Wi-Fi, a data plan, or—for most of us—both.

Christians whose understanding of the world is framed by the Bible can think about our experience as living in a shift from Jerusalem to digital Babylon. These are two of the ways human society is depicted in the Bible, and they endure today as helpful archetypes of civilization.

Jerusalem	Babylon
monoreligious	pluralistic
slower paced	accelerated, frenetic
homogeneous	diverse
central control	open source
sweet and simple	complex and bittersweet
idols: religious pride / false piety	idols: fitting in / not missing out

The pages of Scripture, and the annals of human history, suggest that there are times when faith is at the center and times when faith is pushed to the margins. In digital Babylon, where information (and any *thing* we could ever want or need) is instantly available at the godlike swipe of a finger, Almighty God has been squeezed to the margins. Those of us who long to keep him at the center of our lives constantly fight the centrifugal force of a world spinning us away from him.

This transition—from faith at the center to faith at the margins—is happening in North America and other societies in the cultural West. Our data show widespread, top-to-bottom changes from a Christianized to a post-Christian society.

The tension of displacement felt by many (especially, but not only, white) Christians is this: At a formative time in their lives, they experienced a culture that was more Jerusalem-like. Monotheistic Judeo-Christian faith was at the center, and it dominated with fairly homogenized, white-middle-class values and morals that unashamedly claimed to rely on the Bible for authority. The pace of change was comparatively slow, so there was greater continuity between generational knowledge and experience. Most everyone seemed to agree on what life was about—and in that sense, things felt sweet, simple, and straightforward.

In digital Babylon, on the other hand, the Bible is one of many voices that interpret human experience; it is no longer viewed as the central authority over people and society.[3] Today, if someone unironically drops "the Bible says" in a media interview, they sound as if they have just disembarked from a time machine.

Caught between Cultures

The idol in a Jerusalem-like culture is false piety; people want to appear devout, to look spiritual. Twenty-five years ago, US researchers like those of us at Barna were more likely than today to contend with religious "social desirability bias"—a desire on the part of survey respondents to be perceived as more spiritually engaged than they actually are. That's because there was greater societal pressure to present oneself as a person of faith—even to an anonymous interviewer. That pressure has all but evaporated. It exists now only in pockets of Christian subculture. (From a researcher's point of view, this is excellent news. From a Christian point of view, it's a mixed bag.)

A few years ago, my daughter Annika Kinnaman, who was attending a K–8 Christian school, was on a school bus headed to an outdoor education event. As kids do on a bus with a bunch of other junior high kids, Anni and her friend Kali started up a rousing rendition of "99 Bottles of Beer on the Wall."

One of the teachers, with a disapproving we-don't-sing-about-booze-in-Christian-school scowl, said, "Anni! Beer?"

And sweet Anni said, with 100 percent sincerity, "Oh, I'm sorry. Is it supposed to be 99 bottles of *wine*?"

In Jerusalem, God's people prize appropriate behavior, following rules, and moral purity. The culture of digital Babylon, however, resists the hegemony of a single "right" way of life. Anni got caught in the middle, to awkward and hilarious result.

We often consider our region or city or neighborhood (or Christian school) to be something like a backdrop, the setting against which our—and the other *minor* characters'—lives play out. However, what if we envisioned culture as a character in the story of a person's faith formation?[4] In a play or musical, the set is usually secondary to what the actors say and do, and we have a tendency to think the same about the "set" of our lives. Those who make claims like "There's nothing new about the dropout problem" or "Young adults will return to church when they get married or have kids" perceive culture as a mere backdrop that makes no impact on the thoughts, feelings, relationships, and choices of the characters.

Yet the society we inhabit—the prevailing attitudes, the collective values, the assumptions about human purpose and flourishing, even the tools we use—is more like a character in than the setting of our lives.[5] There is a big difference, for example, between growing up in certain regions of the country and growing up in others in terms of how that socializes us toward or against faith. In other words, culture acts on our stories and on our perceptions of our stories.

Scripture is bursting with vivid characterizations of cities and societies. Jerusalem. Babylon. Sodom. Egypt. Canaan. Galilee. Rome. Laodicea. Nineveh. At the end of the brief book of the Bible named for Jonah, God asks the prophet a rhetorical question: "Shouldn't I feel sorry for such a great city?" (4:11). Nineveh is not a painted canvas background or a cardboard veneer against which Jonah discerns, resists, and is reconciled to his prophetic calling; God cares for every single one of the 120,000-odd Ninevites *and* the Assyrian culture they give birth to. He wants to redeem whole neighborhoods, cities, and societies because they are filled with people made in his image who together create a unique way of being in God's story: a culture.

The Babylon of the Bible is characterized as a culture set against the purposes of God—a human society that glories in pride, power, prestige, and pleasure. Babylon makes appearances throughout the Bible, most notably (and literally) in the story of Daniel. But Babylon is there in the pages of Scripture from beginning to end. From the Tower of Babel, the "first city of man," in the book of Genesis to the final act of God's justice and restoration in Revelation, Babylon is both a place and an archetype of collective human pursuits set in opposition to God.

At least two New Testament writers thought about imperial Rome through this Babylonian framework: Peter in his letters to Christians scattered throughout the empire and John in his apocalyptic vision recorded in the book of Revelation. Like them, exiles in digital Babylon sometimes have a love-hate relationship with the place, like the feeling you have when visiting a big, noisy city in another country; it is intoxicating but exhausting. The complexity can be both fascinating and repellant. Those who love Jesus often feel this tension deeply; we truly appreciate what our society has to offer yet can't help but long for something more safe, more comfortable. A place that feels like home.

The Spirit of Babylon

Empires subjugate weaker nations of the earth using a variety of tactics, not all of which are military. Yes, empires use violence and power to achieve dominance. But military means often go hand in hand with colonial strategies deployed to transform the language, economics, and cultural imagination of conquered peoples. The Jewish elite were captured after Babylonia's military conquest of Judah, forcibly taken to the empire's capital, and subjected to a cultural conquest nearly as devastating as their martial defeat. (The book of Daniel is a vivid account of Babylon's culture-eradication campaign and how some exiles successfully resisted.)

If a literal Babylon were around today, the internet would certainly be in the imperial toolbox—and insofar as we thoughtlessly consume whatever content comes our way, we'd be cheerful participants in our own colonization. Even without a literal empire knocking on our door, many of us are willingly held captive. The infographic on page 26 is one way of envisioning the influence of digital Babylon, held in the balance against spiritual content a typical young person consumes in a given twelve-month period.

The idea of digital colonization may seem extreme, but here is the point: screens inform and connect, but they also distract and entertain. Through screens' ubiquitous presence, Babylon's pride, power, prestige, and pleasure colonize our hearts and minds. Pop culture is a reality filter. Websites, apps, movies, TV, video games, music, social media, YouTube channels, and so on increasingly provide the grid against which we test what is true and what is real. The media and the messages blur the boundary between truth and falsehood. What is real is up for grabs. You've no doubt heard terms like *truthiness, fake news, post-truth,* and *alternative facts.* (Have you also come across the "research" that "proves" Millennials would rather give up their sense of smell than their smartphones? Not a real study.) All these contests to define reality are features of the current Babylonian landscape.

Screens demand our attention. Screens *disciple.*

The power of digital tools and the content they deliver are incredible, and we are the first generation of humans who cannot rely on the earned wisdom of previous generations to help us live with these rapid technological changes. Instead of older adults and traditions, many young people turn to friends and algorithms.

Digital Babylon moves at the pace of fiber optics, and the idol is fitting in and being up to speed. (A twentysomething neighbor recently scoffed that David didn't know a particular Kelly Clarkson song was, "like, really old. It came out earlier this year.") Screens promise more connectedness, but, as researcher Jean Twenge has shown, loneliness, depression, and anxiety among teens have risen alongside widespread adoption of the smartphone.[6] This is the iSelf era, and many young people are crippled by FOMO (the fear of missing out)—not to mention the fear of making the wrong choice, the fear of disappointing people close to them, and the fear of living a substandard life. Talk about anxiety! No wonder so many live depleted, shallow lives, huddled behind their screens consuming personalized content in a futile effort to fill the void.

In a recent study to examine the what, when, and how of faith-sharing in the age of screens, six out of ten Millennials

The Weight of Digital Babylon versus Spiritual Input

"Quietly, using screens and phones for entertainment has become *the* dominant activity of childhood," writes Richard Freed.[7] The power and the pull of screens in the lives of teens and young adults are unreal.

Even using conservative estimates, the typical young person spends nearly twenty times more hours per year using screen-driven media than taking in spiritual content. And for the typical young churchgoer, the ratio is still more than ten times as much cultural content as spiritual intake.

How can we hope to shape the hearts and minds of the next generation with the weight of information stacked against spiritual formation?

Among "typical" fifteen- to twenty-three-year-olds, the estimated number of hours per year are as follows.

Using Screen Media[8]

Typical fifteen- to twenty-three-year-old

Taking in Spiritual Content

Typical fifteen- to twenty-three-year-old churchgoer

Typical fifteen- to twenty-three-year-old

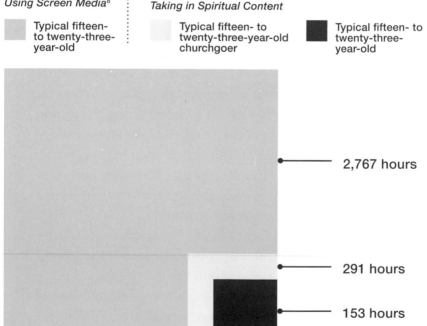

2,767 hours

291 hours

153 hours

Our survey question asked, "How many hours in the last week did you spend focusing on your spirituality, including going to church, reading the Bible, praying, listening to or reading Christian content, or talking about faith?" We used this to estimate an annual total.

told us that "technology and digital interactions make me more careful about how and when I share my faith" (58 percent) and that "people are more likely now than in the past to see me as offensive if I share my faith" (61 percent). Two out of three said that people nowadays are so busy with their screens that they "are more likely to avoid real spiritual conversations" (64 percent).⁹ Of course, screens *can* make sharing faith easier—but those who use them in that way are an exception to the rule.

One reason is that we live in a time and a place characterized by rampant skepticism about Christianity and the Bible. Hyperrationalism and pop-culture atheism undercut belief. A majority of non-Christian youth and young adults are jaded to the appeal of following Jesus. They reject organized religion altogether, especially claims of an exclusive faith like Christianity. Many view the Bible as a book of oppression that is harmful to the minds of its devoted readers. In some influential places, young Christians encounter condescension or downright hostility from their peers, their instructors, and social elites.

In digital Babylon, it is difficult for earnest and sincere people to be taken, well, seriously. A constant drip of snarky YouTube videos and zippy Twitter replies, among other things, erodes any sense of trust in others. How do we persuade young nihilists to put their trust in Jesus—much less in the community of broken saints called the church?

Speaking of church—that's different in digital Babylon too. Christians—even those who are very committed—are busier than ever, attend church less frequently, and have many options for socializing outside a faith community. It is not uncommon for people to attend events and services at multiple churches. Faith-based media is so easily accessible and portable that we've got a whole class of people whom the early church would have found almost unrecognizable: Christian *consumers*. Youth group used to serve as a main social outlet for teens and kids, but it is being replaced by sports and social media. The number of hours connecting, learning, and being discipled in a close-knit church community is now a drop of water in the ocean of content pouring out of their screens.

Much more could be said, but the point is this: we are on the front end of a digital revolution that is tinkering with what it means to be human. And we ain't seen nothin' yet.

We are all residents of digital Babylon.

We are all exiles now.

Resilient Exiles

You Lost Me concludes that the main reason young people drop out of church or fall away from faith is insufficient discipleship. The verdict of that research is that many families and churches have lost their way in terms of effectively discipling the next generation.

We believe many parents, educators, pastors, and other leaders are trying to prepare young Christians for Jerusalem, to keep them safe and well protected for a world they no longer live in. Cultivating faith for exiles means, by contrast, that we—young and old alike—trust that Jesus is Lord even in chaotic, pixelated, no-rules digital Babylon. A Christian identity and a rarely engaged church community are not enough to make someone resistant to the Babylon virus. They never have been.

Peter wrote to Christians in far-flung Roman provinces whom he called "temporary residents."* Check out some of

---

*The NIV and ESV translations, for example, use the word *exiles* for Peter's depiction of these believers in 1 Peter 1:1 and 1 Peter 2:11.

the advice Peter conveyed to the exiles then and there, knowing full well they would be facing significant challenges in the culture he described as "Babylon" (see 1 Pet. 5:13).

> So be truly glad. There is wonderful joy ahead, even though you must endure many trials for a little while. These trials will show that your faith is genuine. It is being tested as fire tests and purifies gold—though your faith is far more precious than mere gold. So when your faith remains strong through many trials, it will bring you much praise and glory and honor on the day when Jesus Christ is revealed to the whole world. (1 Pet. 1:6–7)

> So prepare your minds for action and exercise self-control. Put all your hope in the gracious salvation that will come to you when Jesus Christ is revealed to the world. So you must live as God's obedient children. Don't slip back into your old ways of living to satisfy your own desires. You didn't know any better then. But now you must be holy in everything you do, just as God who chose you is holy. (1 Pet. 1:13–15)

> You are coming to Christ, who is the living cornerstone of God's temple. . . . What's more, you are his holy priests. (1 Pet. 2:4–5)

This is faith for exiles.

We can't go back to Jerusalem. Not yet, at least. So we should plan to stay and figure out how to grow disciples here and now in digital Babylon.

Making Disciples in Digital Babylon

In a previous era, we had some semblance of success with mass-producing disciples. We had big rallies and crusades and whiz-bang events, and many young people came forward to pledge their lives to Christ. But as the growing dropout rate starkly reveals, that approach alone doesn't seem to work here and now as well as it did there and then.

In digital Babylon, faithful, resilient disciples are hand-crafted one life at a time.

Faith for Exiles is a sustained and up-close look at five hand-crafting, soul-shaping practices we've observed over the past ten years, five patterns of intentional behavior we can adopt to guide disciples in the making. But before we dive in, let's build some common ground by thinking together about common goals and suggesting some common language.

We propose that the goal of discipleship today is *to develop Jesus followers who are resiliently faithful in the face of cultural coercion and who live a vibrant life in the Spirit.*

Let's examine the component parts of this definition.

To develop Jesus followers. Our ultimate aim must be to make deep, lasting connections between young people and Jesus, "who initiates and perfects our faith" and endured the cross and its shame to joyfully redeem the world (Heb. 12:2). Those who follow him also undertake his joyful mission of redemption. As a community of faith, we sometimes miss opportunities to propel young people into the mission of Jesus. Millennials and Gen Z are often more willing to be challenged than we are willing to challenge them.*

Who are resiliently faithful in the face of cultural coercion. Resilience is a hot topic in business circles, and for good reason; it's what a person, team, or company needs in order to emerge from inevitable challenges not only intact but also with refined

---

*See the appendix for a breakdown of these generations.

skills and deeper wisdom. In the realm of faith, resilient disciples grow more like Jesus, not in spite of but because of their location in a society that exerts enormous coercive power, as in digital Babylon.

And who live a vibrant life in the Spirit. These Jesus-centered, culture-countering people adopt a way of life that is obviously different from the powerful norms of go-with-the-flow life in the screen age.

Here is the great news: some of these disciples already exist.

Because our main interest in *You Lost Me* was to understand church dropouts, we didn't look closely in that book at those who *stay engaged*. For the research that undergirds *Faith for Exiles*, we took a different approach. Our focus was not those who leave but those who stick around, who find cause as they come of age to make faith a high priority—and find the inner and outer resources to sustain resilient faith in the face of long odds. So this is what we did: using the survey parameters of the *You Lost Me* research—eighteen- to twenty-nine-year-olds with a churchgoing background—we interviewed young adults about their past and present experiences of Christian formation.

To zero in on the most committed young adults, we started by looking for the significant basics of Christian life. These Christians are regularly involved in a worshiping community and have made a personal commitment to Jesus, who they believe was crucified and raised to conquer sin and death. They also strongly affirm that the Bible is the inspired Word of God, which contains truth about the world. For this study, they also had to agree with one or more of the following "exile" statements:

- I want to find a way to follow Jesus that connects with the world I live in.

- God is more at work outside the church than inside, and I want to be a part of that.
- I want to be a Christian without separating myself from the world around me.

How many young Christians meet these criteria? There is a countercultural 10 percent of young Christians whose faith is vibrant and robust. Let's sit with the good news for a minute: from a numbers point of view, this percentage amounts to just under four million eighteen- to twenty-nine-year-olds in the US who follow Jesus and are resiliently faithful. Not only are the most engaged young Christians serious about personal faith and faithfulness, but they are also concerned for and thoughtful about how their faith in Christ intersects meaningfully and missionally with the world around them. In spite of the tensions they feel between church and everyday life, they keep showing up. Three-quarters of them declare a commitment to "help the church change its priorities to be what Jesus intended it to be" (76 percent).

That's resilience.

These are our "exemplars"—those who exemplify the kind of resilient discipleship we believe can flourish in digital Babylon. These sisters and brothers are young adults who model the outcomes hoped for by the community of faith. By getting to know these resilient disciples, we can find out what formation experiences and relationships are most effective for growing resilient faith in exile.

Throughout *Faith for Exiles*, we compare and contrast the practices, beliefs, perspectives, and attitudes of resilient disciples with those of *prodigals* (ex-Christians), *nomads* (church

Four Kinds of Exiles

Resilient faith is not easy to sustain in any context, but it's even harder for young people in digital Babylon. Among today's 18- to 29-year-olds, here is what's happening among those who grew up Christian.

Prodigals (Ex-Christians)
22% Individuals who do not currently identify as Christian despite having attended a Protestant or Catholic church or having considered themselves to be a Christian as a child or teen.

Nomads (Unchurched)
30% People who identify as Christian but have not attended church during the past month. The vast majority of nomads haven't been involved with a church for six months or more.

Habitual Churchgoers
38% Those who describe themselves as Christian and who have attended church at least once in the past month, yet do not meet foundational core beliefs or behaviors associated with being an intentional, engaged disciple.

Resilient Disciples
10% Christ followers who (1) attend church at least monthly and engage with their church more than just attending worship services; (2) trust firmly in the authority of the Bible; (3) are committed to Jesus personally and affirm he was crucified and raised from the dead to conquer sin and death; and (4) express desire to transform the broader society as an outcome of their faith.

N=1,514 U.S. 18–29-year-olds who grew up as Christians | February 2018 | Source: Barna dropouts), and *habitual churchgoers* (those who attend church but don't otherwise qualify under the resilient definition).

All four of these groups have some background in Christianity, and we track all of them throughout this book. The main thrust of our efforts, however, is to better understand resilient disciples. They represent the leading lights of young adult Christianity— not because they are perfect but because they exemplify a full-bodied experience of following Jesus that we should all hope to emulate. Most of their Christianized peers do not.

Five Practices of Resilient Faith

As part of our research with young resilient disciples, we kept probing the data to discern the story behind their resilience. If these are the kinds of Christians we hope to raise, support, and emulate, what can we learn from them? What makes them tick? What practices seem to distinguish these powerful examples of faith from the norm?

Our research shows that, in the face of a coercive, spirit-depleting, screen-obsessed society, cultivating the following five practices helps to form resilient faith. Again, these are not simple formulas; they are guidelines and guardrails for the formation of the soul. Think of these as the spiritual scaffolding around a young soul that enables the Holy Spirit to access the life inside, or the trellis that supports a growing disciple's branches as their roots sink deep enough to sustain them.

- Practice 1: To form a resilient identity, experience intimacy with Jesus.
- Practice 2: In a complex and anxious age, develop the muscles of cultural discernment.

- Practice 3: When isolation and mistrust are the norms, forge meaningful, intergenerational relationships.

- Practice 4: To ground and motivate an ambitious generation, train for vocational discipleship.

- Practice 5: Curb entitlement and self-centered tendencies by engaging in countercultural mission.

These five practices summarize a decade of work, research, thinking, and listening to discover hopeful ways forward. You can read the appendix for a detailed description of our methodology, but check out pages 36–37 for a big picture of these five practices and some of the components they include.

■ ■ ■

As I drove home from Berkeley, Mark called me from the other side of the country—New York City, to be exact. He and his wife, Jade, had just dropped off *their* daughter, Skye, for her first year of college in the fashion program at Parsons School of Design. "We've been having some great conversations with our daughter," Mark said as we compared notes. We laughed at the symmetry of our experiences and our lame last-minute parenting.

Now Emily is in the San Francisco area aspiring to a life in science (unless she decides to pursue one of her other myriad interests), while Skye is a continent away in New York City preparing for a career in the arts. Like generations of students before them, they must make their way as Christians in unfamiliar territory. But unlike any previous group of young believers, they are also residents of someplace entirely new: digital Babylon.

What Resilience Looks Like

Experiencing Jesus

My relationship with Jesus brings me deep joy and satisfaction. **89%**

Jesus speaks to me in a way that is relevant to my life. **83%**

Worship is a lifestyle, not just an event. **91%**

Cultural Discernment

The Bible teaching I receive in my church is relevant to my life. **86%**

In my church, I regularly receive wisdom for how to live faithfully in a secular world. **70%**

At church I get wisdom for how the Bible applies to my life. **86%**

Meaningful Relationships

The church is a place where I feel I belong. **88%**

There is someone in my life who encourages me to grow spiritually. **85%**

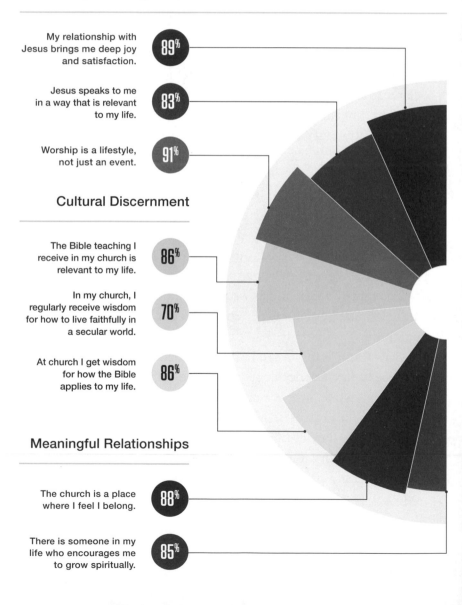

As we explored the profile of resilient disciples ages eighteen to twenty-nine, we discovered five sets of characteristics that distinguish them from other young churchgoers. The percentages below reflect the proportion of resilient disciples—the exemplars in our study—who responded affirmatively to each statement, far ahead of their Christian peers.

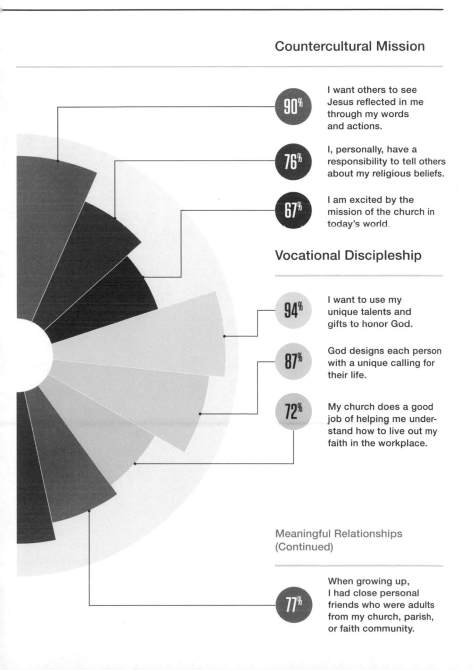

Countercultural Mission

90% I want others to see Jesus reflected in me through my words and actions.

76% I, personally, have a responsibility to tell others about my religious beliefs.

67% I am excited by the mission of the church in today's world.

Vocational Discipleship

94% I want to use my unique talents and gifts to honor God.

87% God designs each person with a unique calling for their life.

72% My church does a good job of helping me understand how to live out my faith in the workplace.

Meaningful Relationships (Continued)

77% When growing up, I had close personal friends who were adults from my church, parish, or faith community.

To Form a Resilient Identity, Experience Intimacy with Jesus

Experiencing Jesus means clearing religious clutter for closeness with and joy in Christ.

ime for a quick Kinnaman flashback. My daughter Emily is eight. I am lying in bed next to her, tucking her in for the night. After a long conversation, ranging from favorite Disney movies to preferred methods of assembling puzzles to the life and times of a sweet little girl, we turn to spiritual topics. Her questions are good ones, and after a while, I ask her one of my own.

"Hey, Emily, do you believe in Jesus?"

Emily exclaims, "Yes!"

"Why do you believe in him?"

"Because we read about him in the Bible."

"That's a good answer. Do you have any other reasons?"

After a long and thoughtful pause, Emily says, "Dad, do you remember when we prayed for that family, about whether they should join our home group? And then we saw them in Home Depot, and it gave us a chance to ask them to come?"

"Yes, I remember."

"That was a miracle, Dad. That's why I believe in Jesus."

Even to young souls, experiencing Jesus at an intimate level helps reinforce who they are and what they believe.

■ ■ ■

The first practice of resilient discipleship we uncovered in our research among exemplar, young adults (the group we labeled *resilient disciples*) is a transformational experience of Jesus. Most Americans say they are Christians, but few follow that up with deep, heart-level, life-directing commitments. This is true of all generations, and it remains true of young adults.

Looking at the full spectrum of young adults' experiences with Christianity—from prodigals and nomads (the churchless) to habitual churchgoers and resilient disciples (churchgoers)—helps us make sense of the drop-off spots on the road to resilience. It turns out that calling oneself a Christian represents a very low bar. About two out of three eighteen- to twenty-nine-year-olds in the US say they are Christian (a notable statistic, given all our hand-wringing about the rise of the nones). According to the study we conducted specifically for this book, 100 percent of nomads, habituals, and resilients identify as Christian; we sorted them into those buckets *because* they ticked the "Christian" box. Prodigals, on the other hand, consider themselves to be something else, and usually that's religiously unaffiliated.

We also inquired how young adults would comfortably describe their faith to others, not just how they would label themselves. The vast majority of resilient disciples and habitual churchgoers say they would use phrases like "a Christian" or "a follower of Jesus" to describe themselves to other people. More than half of nomads and even some prodigals also appear comfortable using these self-descriptions.[1]

You can see where we are headed: It's easy for young adults to call themselves Christian. It is much less common, however, for young people with Christian experience to find their identity in Jesus.

You may have heard of the metaphor of "inoculating" people to the gospel. In a medical scenario, of course, inoculation involves exposing someone to a virus so their cells produce a natural antibody to guard against future full exposure. Sadly, this is an apt description of what happens with Jesus in many young lives. Having been exposed to Christianity, people form patterns and habits that resist deeper faith. These faith antibodies are part of the natural human bent away from God but are also exacerbated by Christian structures that enable superficial, skin-deep spirituality.

Look at the data in table 1. Resilient disciples are much more likely to agree strongly with statements about Jesus that other Christian segments tend to reject. For example, nine out of ten resilient disciples strongly agree that "living in relationship with Jesus is the only way to find fulfillment in life," that "my relationship with Jesus brings me deep joy and satisfaction," and that "following Jesus shapes my whole life: body, mind, heart, and soul." More than eight out of ten resilient disciples firmly agree that "my relationship with Jesus impacts the way I live my life every day."

What's so remarkable about resilient disciples is that they truly exhibit a higher level of intimacy with Jesus than other young adults raised in the faith. (Resilient disciples aren't perfect by any stretch. That's a theme to which we will return. Resilient disciples, and the churches in which they are planted, still have lots of room to grow.) It's heartbreaking to find that only about half of habitual churchgoers—young adults who

Table 1. It Is Easy to Say You Are a Christian—but Less Common to Find Joy in Jesus	Prodigals/ Ex-Christians ✗	Nomads/ Unchurched ◉	Habitual Churchgoers ⌂	Resilient Disciples ■
Identifying as Christian				
Right now, what religious faith do you consider yourself to be? Christian*	0%	100%	100%	100%
Which of the following phrases best fits how you would describe your faith to others (completely or mostly)?				
A follower of Jesus		61%	79%	97%
A Christian		58%	81%	95%
The Centrality of Jesus in Life (% strongly agree)				
I believe living in relationship with Jesus is the only way to find fulfillment in life.		21%	49%	89%
My relationship with Jesus brings me deep joy and satisfaction.		25%	48%	90%
Following Jesus shapes my whole life: body, mind, heart, and soul.		24%	51%	88%
My relationship with Jesus impacts the way I live my life every day.		23%	49%	86%

N = 1,514 US 18- to 29-year-olds who grew up as Christians
Source: Barna, February 2018
*This question was used in part to distinguish prodigals from the other three segments.

attend church with regularity—strongly agree with straightforward questions about Jesus. How is it possible to show up week after week, year after year, without believing and experiencing Jesus more fully? Habitual churchgoers should top the list of churches' discipleship priorities; many of these young Christians are primed and ready for a deeper experience of (and commitment to) Christ.

It is easy to call oneself a Christian but much less common to find deep joy in Jesus. That conclusion is where our first practice begins. *The first practice of resilient discipleship in digital Babylon is clearing religious clutter to experience intimacy with Jesus.*

In the pages that follow, we're going to show just how cluttered the path has become. In some cases, it's like hoarders for Jesus. The living Lord is crammed into the small spaces of mental attics alongside all sorts of other accumulated ideas and idols. Unfortunately, churches sometimes sanction the extra baggage, which Jesus warned could happen: "For you crush people with unbearable religious demands, and you never lift a finger to ease the burden" (Luke 11:46).

From the data in table 2, two themes emerge. First, resilient disciples express a feeling of intimacy with God, closeness that frequently seems lacking in the experience of habituals, nomads, and prodigals. Statements like "Jesus understands what my life is like these days" and "Reading the Bible makes me feel closer to God" capture this feeling. Resilience is felt at a deep, emotional level.

Second, resilient disciples experience conversational intimacy with Jesus. More than four out of five strongly agree with the statement "Jesus speaks to me in a way that is relevant to my life." Fewer than half of habituals feel this kind of connection, and the percentages are, as expected, much lower among nomads and prodigals. Prayer is a "vibrant part" of resilient disciples' lives, and it includes "listening to God."

Taken together, the data tells us that resilient disciples build their identity in Jesus. This is rare. In digital Babylon, as in

Table 2. What Builds Resilient Disciples? Intimacy and Conversation with Jesus	Prodigals/ Ex-Christians	Nomads/ Unchurched	Habitual Churchgoers	Resilient Disciples
Experiencing Intimacy with God (% strongly agree)				
Worship is a lifestyle, not just an event.	20%	33%	50%	91%
Jesus has deeply transformed my life.	8%	31%	46%	87%
Reading the Bible makes me feel closer to God.	10%	21%	44%	87%
Jesus understands what my life is like these days.	13%	36%	51%	79%
Regularly experience at church: the reality of God's presence.	13%	23%	43%	75%
Regularly experience at church: guidance for how to grow the fruit of the Spirit.	10%	14%	34%	70%
Talking with Jesus (% strongly agree)				
I am reenergized when I spend time with Jesus.	10%	23%	46%	87%
Jesus speaks to me in a way that is relevant to my life.	10%	31%	43%	83%
Listening to God is a big part of my prayer life.	12%	21%	48%	78%
Prayer does not feel like a formal routine but a vibrant part of my life.	11%	17%	39%	64%

N = 1,514 US 18- to 29-year-olds who grew up as Christians
Source: Barna, February 2018

other societies, figuring out who we are is one of the epic struggles of being human. This battle to define identity is one reason disciple making is so difficult today.

The Search for Identity

Human beings are unique among creation in part because we undergo a constant search for identity. We all want to know, *Who am I, really?* It is one of humanity's timeless questions; the search for answers has driven men and women from the very beginning. It is also an *ageless* question; that is, we return to the search on and off throughout our lives.

We look for answers to this deep-seated question in all sorts of people, places, and things

brands
bands
clothes
celebrities
sports we follow
sports we play
where we're from
where we love to go
those we admire
our work
our sexuality

And on and on. Human beings blend their identities from a menu of ingredients, like a me-shaped Frappuccino of wants, needs, desires, and self-perceptions.

In digital Babylon, our screens grant us access to a plethora of identity-forming tools, communities, and adventures. Think about it. Before the internet, if you were really into Swedish death metal and Picasso-inspired decoupage (we see that hand!), it's unlikely you had a community of connoisseurs with whom to share, learn, and be. But now, as a proud resident of digital Babylon, you have nearly instant access to your fellow Viking metalheads and Mod Podgers, who can help you become your best head-banging, Mod-Podging self.

Algorithms that run the apps and search results on our magical devices anticipate and guide the trajectory of our search, providing helpful suggestions for our identity-forming efforts. We will delve deeper into the power of algorithms in the next chapter, but for now, here's an example. Like a good friend, Netflix recommends shows you might like based on shows you've already watched. Facebook suggests news you will find interesting based on past behavior. How thoughtful of those computer-driven preference models! Digital screens, and the algorithms that orchestrate their flickering pixels, know you better than you know yourself.

Actually, the marketers behind the algorithms know who they would *like* you to be so they can sell you things. Companies understand better than ever before what it means to market and position themselves as a lifestyle brand, whether they are selling surfboards, technology, outdoorsiness, home renovation, craft coffee, or cooking.

Almost everything we buy carries a latent message: the people who purchase such-and-such are [*fill in the blank*]. Walk into an REI and you encounter clear messages about the identity and lifestyle of outdoors enthusiasts. Same with an Apple store. Everything from the layout, display design, and font choices communicate something about the people who use the company's products. The next time you pick up a consumer catalog or watch a YouTube before-the-video ad, pause to think, *What is the identity being sold here?* What we consume stakes a claim on who we are, and that is the stuff of identity.

Another digital Babylon distinctive is that being different and unique—reflected in the oft-repeated mantra "You do you"—is among the highest priorities in the quest for identity. Our society deifies the individual's search for self-expression. Ironically, however, most of us end up looking like the crowd we want to be a part of; the apparent value placed on self-expression is actually driven by someone else's preferences. Even when we think we're marching to our own beat, we've got an unseen drummer in our heads, keeping time and making claims on our identity.

Brand Me

It is more than possible to be and raise resilient disciples in digital Babylon, but we need to understand what's at stake when it comes to identity. We must grasp how its essence is being redefined, even distorted, here in exile.

One of those distortions is a trend we could describe as "elective identity," the idea that people can and should define their own identity, that the individual—there's that word again—is the ultimate arbiter of what is true about herself or himself.[2] Most people today, including Christians, believe identity can be discovered and decided on by the individual. A perfectly terrible example is the degree to which Christians embrace a pop culture moral code that starts and ends with "me." A majority of Christians have succumbed to wrong-headed ideas such as:

- You discover the truth about yourself by looking inside yourself.
- You can believe whatever you want as long as those beliefs don't affect society.
- You should pursue the things you desire most.

Collectively, our society says that our choices define our identity. But that is only partly true. It's true enough that our choices inform what we make of our lives. Certainly, we believe that God created human beings with agency to make choices. But we must persuade young exiles that the *truest* thing about humans is what our Creator says about us: that we are created with essential worth and dignity as children crafted in his image and that following his Son, Jesus, restores his image in us, which was broken as a result of human rebellion.

Contrary to the Creator's intentions, human identity is under a full-scale rebrand in digital Babylon. Personal screens reinforce the notion of elective identity by giving us daily, even hourly, chances to present a self-selected, carefully filtered, curated version of ourselves to friends and followers. Social media, for all its promises to connect people, also feeds our worst individualist, brand-making impulses by asking us to present (or perform) our "personal brand guidelines" on Facebook, Twitter, and Instagram. Every day the message is reinforced: you get to—you must—define who you are.

Questions of identity are major themes on a variety of levels for today's young adults and teens. Take, for example, the arena of gender identity. In Barna's study of Gen Z, we discovered that today's teenagers are much more open to the idea that gender is determined by how you *feel*, not by your birth sex. One out of three teens believes this is true. Seven out of ten say it's acceptable to be born one gender and feel like another, while two out of five contend it's okay for someone to change their body to become another gender.[3]

The fact that some people experience questions surrounding their gender is not new. What *is* new is the pervasive sense that, because it happens to *some* individuals, gender must be something *everyone* has to wrestle to the ground for themselves. There is a ubiquitous sense of live and let live, of you-do-youism, in the quest of young generations to define their identity—which is at odds with how the Scriptures portray what it means to be human.

In digital Babylon, we are all encouraged, even expected, to carefully curate what our own individual brand is: Brand Me. These fluid identities we create and take on do not stand the test of time and, like the house built on sand, collapse instantly when the storm arrives.

But there's one thing even more disruptive to forming a resilient identity than creating our own version of "me," and that is creating our own version of Jesus.

Brand Jesus

One sparkling spring day in Southern California, David was talking with a group of ministry interns. One of the young women kept asking questions and making comments that prominently featured the word *me*, such as "But that's not what this passage of Scripture is saying to *me*."

49

The cultural crosscurrents of branding and individualism exert tremendous pull on today's young Christians. In one Barna study, we discovered that there has been a shift in American Christianity toward the notion that discipleship is a solo effort, that the best way to grow spiritually is on your own.[4] This trend echoes the cultural refrains of the moment: *You do you. Find yourself by looking within. Speak your truth.* Young Christians are deeply affected by our cultural climate too, and we shouldn't be surprised. But we must find a better way of making them resilient.

You can see what's at stake, even when it comes to perceptions of our spiritual choices. In an era of elective identity, Jesus doesn't choose us. He is the ultimate opt in. (You can almost see the pop-up on your browser: "To continue on Jesus.com, we require that you accept cookies. Do you agree to these terms?")

Too often, churches and Christian families have capitulated to the culture's terms in this regard. And we believe this massive mistake has led to failing discipleship.

> The church has responded to the identity pressures of our culture by offering young people a Jesus "brand experience" rather than facilitating a transformational experience to find their identity in the person and work of Jesus.

First, we've been complicit in presenting a Jesus to compete *at the same level* as other affiliations and affinities. Jesus is your cool BFF, your partner in adventure who wants to be tagged in your selfies and help you live your best life. And he can be co-branded with just about anything! Being a Christian is not meaningfully different from participating in the branded culture of our times—it is a transaction equivalent to following a band on Instagram, attending the concerts, and wearing the swag. Jesus is just one more brand competing for our loyalty.

But mere fans of Brand Jesus are not at all resilient under the pressures of life in exile.

A second way we've capitulated is to expect too little. The church is one of the least demanding environments for young people, in terms of what they are asked to do mentally and emotionally and of what is expected of them when it comes to serving and giving. We're just so happy to have them there! Yet one of the most hopeful findings in our research is this: young exemplar Christians are more willing to be challenged than the church is willing to challenge them. This means they expect to be asked to do more but in reality experience a faith community that doesn't ask all that much of them. David has a missionary friend who said he receives the most teen interest in joining their mission organization *not* when he promises a good life or talks about the cool places they might live but when he tells them that the mission field will require everything of them, perhaps even their lives.

Undertaking a radical, life-altering mission (see Practice 5) is what our young generations crave, but instead, we take everything, from our worship services to what's required of a Christian, and mold it into the shape of comfort and entertainment. They *want* to get their hands dirty. Churches, schools, and families that ask *more* of young men and women and give them meaningful opportunities to be engaged are indispensable to their spiritual growth.

Brands don't ask all that much from their fans. Jesus asks us to give *everything*.

The fact that many parents don't model spiritual vitality at home also contributes to the problem. In addition, the professionalization of ministry is partly to blame; we've become really good at doing ministry *to* people. And a major complaint of the next generation is that the church often feels too slick, too produced, too businesslike.

If Brand Jesus adds to the identity clutter rather than forming resilient disciples, what's the alternative?

People grapple with all kinds of answers to—and with many ways to find answers for—the big questions in life. The best answers, we believe, come from historic, orthodox Christianity and are best (though inadequately) expressed in the community of redeemed saints called the church. We believe humanity's timeless questions are fully answered not by our habits as consumers or by looking inside ourselves but through faith in Christ. We find in Jesus the truest answer to who we are (children of God) and what we are meant to be (representatives of God's glory).

As for the best way to find an answer to the perennial question *Who am I, really?* we believe nothing can compare with actually following the real Jesus.

But clearing the identity and religious clutter to become actual followers of the real Jesus is a path too rarely taken.

Experiencing Jesus in Exile

Exiles throughout Scripture participated in an identity-forming way of life—at least, the rare exiles who are remembered for surviving and thriving did. The other kind of exiles, the ones who succumbed to cultural pressure, didn't have annals written about them. Exiles who remain faithful to their true home are important during times when society under-goes fundamental change, especially when the broader social stresses to conform reach a fever pitch. They play a critical role in reminding us how to stay on the path of faithfulness.

Modern notions of individuals and identity are so different from those of ancient history that we have to be careful about letting our current understanding of these concepts inform our interpretation of Scripture. Still, there are things we can learn from the exiles of old that have bearing on our present reality.

Daniel was a young Hebrew when his people were uprooted from their homeland and made to serve a powerful new king-dom in Babylon. Most of what we know about Daniel and the supporting actors in his story (Shadrach, Meshach, and Abednego) arises from their resilience in the face of pressure to conform. They dared to stand up to the powers of the empire for the sake of their God. Yet we often miss the subtle realities at the heart of this story. As modern readers, we underestimate the indoctrinating power that Babylon wielded. In chapter 1 of Daniel's story, we learn that these young men were taught the language and literature of Babylon for three years. They were assigned names based on the identities of Babylonian gods and goddesses. They were asked to form their tastes in the manner of the rich and decadent diet provided by the royal house.

These were some of the tools Babylon used in the effort to turn these young Hebrew men into young Babylonian men.

Daniel and his peers, instead of ingratiating themselves into the indoctrinating systems of their captors, waited on God, lis-tened for his voice, and became a conduit to express his power. Throughout the story of Daniel, we read about young exiles who allowed their habits of devotion to God to define them. And those habits made all the difference to their resilience.

We've baked this notion of resilience into our definition of discipleship: developing Jesus followers who are resiliently faithful in the face of cultural coercion and who live a vibrant life in the Spirit. Here are six research-based insights we've uncovered how a resilient identity can be nurtured in Christian disciples.

Experience Jesus Together

In our qualitative interviews, we discovered that people don't learn to follow Jesus simply by having lots of great head knowledge about him (although having the right beliefs matters, as we'll see). Experiencing Jesus is found along a relational pathway with family, friends, and other people who love and experience Jesus. We are loved into loving Jesus.

Arthur, in our interviews, said he makes himself available to young adults and thinks of himself as a "living epistle, not simply telling them about Jesus but allowing them to see and experience him through my life." Another interviewee, Brett, said he most often experiences Jesus with young adults in a "family-type environment, where they feel safe and known." This includes having young people over for dinner and letting them "share stories honestly and openly of their faith, doubts, and struggles. We find that having young people in our home, around our dinner table, sharing our stories, and praying for one another, can foster effective discipleship."

Jim told our researchers a specific story about spending time listening to a young woman's experience with a bad leader on a church mission trip. "I think we owe honesty to young people. Hearing from her directly and listening intently helped me to redirect her frustration with the flaws in her leader toward the person of Jesus." This notion of a healthy relationship is something we will come back to in Practice 3, but it's worth noting here that having functional human relationships, rather than dysfunctional ones, is one way to clear the clutter and help people experience Jesus.

Families help their individual members discover and maintain their resilient identity. Resilients frequently, though not exclusively, grow up in homes where their parents', grandparents', and other adults' faith is vibrant. A cautionary note, however: in exile, family faith is becoming less influential, and thus passing it on is less automatic. The gravitational pull of digital Babylon is stronger than the memory of Jerusalem.

Still, when older adults model deep ways of following Jesus, young people notice—and not only when these people are their parents. Just as unmarried Christian adults need an extended family of faith, young disciples need attention and care from multiple adult gardeners in order to thrive in exile and to discover their identity.

How can we become households of faith that move beyond habitual churchgoing into engaged discipleship?

Navigate by the True North of Christ

The clear and present danger of inoculating young Christians to the gospel should weigh heavy on our hearts and minds. Just as we should plan carefully to avoid the *external* coercion of secularism in digital Babylon, we must take care not to succumb to the *internal* pressures of a falsely Christianized context. We must diligently search our churchified systems and purge them of inoculating effects. Jesus warned that many would do great works in his name but that he wouldn't

55

even recognize them (Matt. 7:21–23). And this: What does it profit a person to gain the whole world but lose their soul? (Matt. 16:26). Jesus repeatedly warned the religious leaders of his day that they were responsible even for the unintended consequences of their decisions and actions.

In other words, we have to redirect people from Brand Jesus to the Jesus of the Gospels.

Jesus's spotlight on motivations should give us a much-needed dose of humility. What are we trying to accomplish, and to what end? Are we inadvertently pushing a Brand Jesus experience? Are we allowing companies, political parties, nations, or brands to recommend, suggest, guide, or even define our identity?

The answer is almost certainly yes. Idol making is the way of human life; thus, we should continually ask Jesus to reveal these blind spots to us, and then we should repent of them.

If, in trying to build our ministries, churches, and impact, we have contributed to the inoculation of a generation, how can we repent? First, we have to redesign our ministry models to generate the kind of transformation we know disciple making requires. This might mean giving up salaries, staff, size, and status so that we can go after a meaningful relationship with Jesus of Nazareth. We have to look for ways to offer deep explorations of Christ and not just go through the motions of church. As church leaders, making Jesus our true north means prioritizing these eager followers who are so passionate for Jesus—not running a spiritual club.

In addition, we must speak courageously when Christians co-opt the world's way of doing things. Pushing Brand Jesus is capitulating to digital Babylon's terms. What we say to one another and how we say it matters. For instance, when we see or hear Christians talking about living your truth, achieving your dreams, or you doing you, we need to gently but firmly correct those Brand Jesus notions. The new moral code says the individual is the center of the moral universe, but Christianity teaches that we orient ourselves by external sources of authority (the Holy Spirit, the Scriptures, the church, etc.).

When Christians capitulate to the zeitgeist of cultural norms—if we cannot articulate a countercultural biblical morality, for example—we leave the next generation immunodeficient. That is the very essence of inoculating young people. We leave them open to lapsing in faith, because why should they resist a culturally derived moralism masquerading as Christianity?

One of the keys to helping the next generation genuinely experience Jesus is to make sure the Christiany things we surround them with don't keep them away from him. We are responsible even for unintended consequences.

How, then, can we orient our compass away from Brand Jesus toward the true north of the living Lord?

Fearlessly Ask the Big Questions of Life (and Find Answers in Jesus)

The deep search for identity—*Who am I, really?*—is going on in each person, and no one should accept shallow answers. This is but one of a dozen or so fundamental, aching questions that vex humanity. Human beings often find untrue or incomplete answers to these big questions—or increasingly avoid them altogether with streamed entertainment, virtual vacations, and an endless barrage of sensory delights.

Following Jesus means finding the ultimate answer to these questions in the person and work of Jesus. To be more precise, in the Trinity. If there is a real Father, Son, and Holy Spirit, their life anchors our search for truth—especially the search for truth about ourselves. But the entire process begins by creating space where fellow Christians feel they have permission to ask the big questions.

- Questions of identity: *Who am I, really? Where do I find my truest self?* We are children of God, adopted into his family through Jesus. What the Scriptures say about us is the truest thing about us.

- Questions about how to live: *How should I live in today's world? Do my choices matter?* The Holy Spirit willingly and cheerfully gives wisdom and discernment to those who ask. Following Jesus redefines the search for how to live.

- Questions about intimacy and relationships: *Am I loved? Who are my friends? Does anyone care about me?* As part of the community of Jesus, we bear one another's burdens and experience love and intimacy.

- Questions of meaning and purpose: *Does my life matter? Am I made for something?* The Creator made us in his image to love him, other people, and creation, especially through our gifts and our work.

- Questions about legacy and significance: *Can I make a difference? What really matters? What counts for a life well lived?* Since reality is both physical and spiritual, and Jesus has been given authority over all things, we participate with him as restorers of both physical and spiritual dimensions of life, doing good to and in the world and blessing others.

Effective ministry and preaching excavate questions that lie at the heart of human experience and help people grapple with the answers found in Jesus. His responses reverberate through the centuries.

> Love the LORD your God with all your heart, all your soul, all your strength, and all your mind. . . . Love your neighbor as yourself. (Luke 10:27)

> I have come so that [people] may have life, and have it to the full. (John 10:10 NIV)

> If the Son sets you free, you are truly free. (John 8:36)

We are bombarded in digital Babylon, with unprecedented force and frequency, by conflicting, chaotic messages about what matters and how to live. The latest blog post, the newest music, the most popular television show, and even the news all do their level best to convince us we should care and what to do about it (buy something, usually). These messages are constantly changing. We must anchor our search for identity in something deeper and truer, which means we must, like Daniel and his comrades, learn the habits of devotion. We must repeat, to ourselves and to one another, what the Bible says about us. The idea of identity is relatively new language for the way we humans conceive of our experience, and the Bible invites us to consider human reality in an ancient-but-relevant way. What a gift!

> There is now no condemnation for those who are in Christ Jesus. (Rom. 8:1 NIV)

Anyone who belongs to Christ has become a new person. (2 Cor. 5:17)

We are God's masterpiece. He has created us anew in Christ Jesus, so we can do the good things he planned for us long ago. (Eph. 2:10)

Above all else, guard your heart, for everything you do flows from it. (Prov. 4:23 NIV)

Resilient disciples accept and act on orthodox beliefs about Jesus. Right beliefs aren't the whole picture of following him, but without them, we eventually head in the wrong direction.

How can we help young Christians center their experience of Jesus on asking life's deepest questions and discovering the truest answers?

We can start this process by creating space for questions, engaging our younger generations in meaningful mentor relationships (more on this in Practice 3), and facilitating discussions in which the worst examples of Brand Jesus are exposed for what they are: a shallow, get-rich-quick kind of gospel.

Don't Rush a Decision to Follow Jesus

One surprise in our findings is the average (median) age of conversion. We expected to find that resilient disciples have been Christians the longest, but we in fact discovered nearly the opposite. The age of conversion *increases* across the continuum, from prodigals to resilients. The average age for making a decision to follow Jesus is eight for prodigals and nomads, nine for habitual churchgoers, and eleven for resilient disciples.

It appears that resilient disciples are more likely to make a decision to follow Jesus when they know what they are signing up for. This speaks to the importance of all phases of ministry, whether to children, tweens, teens, or young adults. It puts an exclamation point after the necessity of effective ministry to middle school and high school students (not that you were doubting it) and gives parents and pastors a little breathing room. It is never too late (or too early) for young people to experience Jesus.

While we're talking about averages, a crucial reminder is that every story matters. We must honor that each person develops and hears from the Holy Spirit in their own time and way. Let's take care not to be automated in our discipleship processes or expectations.

How can we create effective partnerships and strategies for Jesus-centered ministry across developmental ages in a way that helps people discover and maintain a resilient Christian identity that finds its source in intimacy with Christ?

Get Close and Stay Close to Jesus

Resilient young disciples are hungry for Jesus in their lives, much more so than other young Christians. Looking back at table 1, do you notice the degree to which resilient disciples say they find deep joy and satisfaction in their relationship with Jesus? It is one of their distinguishing characteristics. They describe their relationship with Jesus in very intimate terms. They "feel" close to him.

Worshiping God and experiencing his presence emerge over and over as key priorities for resilient disciples. These activities are about connecting with God. Resilients engage in spiritual activities out of a desire to experience a holy and transcendent God, while other young adult Christians are more likely to be motivated by what's-in-religion-for-me impulses.

Resilients also feel compelled to grow in faith. (Consider table 2 again.) Seven out of ten say their experience at church provides "guidance for how to grow the fruit of the Spirit." Statistical analysis indicates this factor is particularly important in predicting a resilient disciple. Habitual churchgoers, on the other hand, tend to go to church out of tradition.

What might amount to mundane activities also seem to find greater resonance among engaged disciples. "Reading the Bible makes me feel closer to God" is a firm sentiment of nearly nine out of ten young exemplars. They tend to think "God first" in their pursuit of spiritual activities, and they also feel an increased sense that "Jesus understands what my life is like these days."

We also found that resilient disciples are highly likely to say that Jesus speaks to them. In the research for *You Lost Me*, we were struck by the fact that one of the predictors of sticking with faith was the experience of communicating with God, so we explored this further in the new research—and were not surprised to find that agreeing "Jesus speaks to me in a way that is relevant to my life" is highly correlated with resilient disciples. They also say that prayer does not feel like a formal routine but "a vibrant part of my life" and that "listening to God is a big part of my prayer life."

By teaching our young people more about prayer and facilitating times for them to experience the intimacy it brings with Christ, we will further solidify their identity in Christ. One leader we interviewed commented, "There's never been a theoretical experience of Jesus. All that is an abstraction.

When I've seen young adults experience him, it's unmistakable. When the young adult (or any of us) is given space and intention to pay attention to what is happening around them and in them, God is already there."

Go to Church, but Don't Expect Churchgoing Alone to Bring Intimacy with Christ

Sometimes we mistake being on the path—say, attending church—for making active progress as a disciple. But many young people (and older adults, for that matter) are dutiful churchgoers while remaining otherwise spiritually inert. Church involvement is a necessary but insufficient condition for resilient discipleship. This is a powerful finding.

It is difficult, if not downright impossible, to shape hearts and minds with only a few hours a week to work with. Perhaps an analogy will bring this into sharp focus. Let's say you show up at a home improvement store and stand in the paint aisle every week for five years straight. You even attend a couple of special demonstrations by the experts in the orange aprons.

That doesn't make you a painter.

As shown in the previous chapter, about two out of every five young adults who were raised as Christians are now habitual churchgoers (38 percent). They attend a church with some frequency but are missing critical elements of belief, practice, or passion for their faith. Another three out of ten are nomads (30 percent) who rarely attend church or engage in their faith but are still satisfied to wear Brand Jesus. And finally, more than one-fifth turn into prodigals (22 percent), people who no longer identify with Christianity in adulthood.

The overall dropout rate (from 59 to 64 percent in less than a decade) is a sobering referendum on the effectiveness of our ministry to kids and teens. The research suggests we too easily mistake the starting point for the destination, oversimplifying Christianity to mere decisionism. Beginning the journey in Jesus, or making a commitment to become a Christian, is often seen as true transformation in Christ. We make no equivocation that a decision to follow Jesus is vitally important. It is the *beginning* of the most important thing any of us can do in this life, but it cannot stop there. If our young people are going to thrive in digital Babylon, they have to move beyond familiarity with Jesus into a place of intimacy.

We believe right orthodoxy is so crucial that we've defined resilient disciples in part based on their *belief* that Jesus conquered sin and death by virtue of his death and resurrection. It matters that young people understand and trust the core orthodox teaching of Jesus's life, work, death, and resurrection.

But nearly nine out of ten habitual churchgoers also believe that Jesus defeated sin and death. The vast majority of nomads (82 percent) and even one-third of prodigals agree. Do you see that it is not merely *believing* in the truth that transforms?

Today's disciples and the process of discipleship require greater intentionality, greater thoughtfulness. How clear is your picture of what it means to disciple someone?

Resilience and Godward Rhythms

One of the keys to developing resilient faith and experiencing Jesus is growing young people's belief that a real God really speaks to us—that he has something unique to say to our hearts and destinies. This is a theme that runs throughout our studies among Millennials of the last decade, and it's certainly a theme that resounds in Scripture. Hearing from God is also one of the defining characteristics of exiles in the Bible.

We must help this emerging generation hear and respond to the voice of Jesus in their lives.

Let's commit ourselves to helping young people develop a theology and a practice of hearing from, listening to, and talking with God. There are many wonderful examples in the Bible (for example, Daniel, the most famous exile) as well as a multitude of heroes of the faith who demonstrate this crucial resilience-building mind-set and habit.

David's pastor, Britt Merrick, said something recently about intentionally cultivating openness to God. The way we do that, he said, is to live by regular "Godward rhythms" that open us up to his voice and work in our lives. Together, let's cultivate Godward rhythms: spiritual habits and a heartfelt expectation that God will come and speak to us. We can trust that God speaks and that he often does so most clearly through the pages of the Bible. He also talks to us through the voice of the Holy Spirit in our thoughts and feelings and through the counsel of brothers and sisters in our lives.

Hearing from God isn't some spooky, transcendental thing in which our eyes glaze over and God takes over our bodies. The profile of resilient disciples shows us that it's much more natural; it's an everyday reliance on God and dependence on his presence. It's cultivating a soft heart to God's leading.

One of the classic Bible stories on the subject is recorded in 1 Samuel 3. After the boy prophet Samuel is consecrated to the temple by his mother, Hannah, he's placed under the tutelage of a calcified and corrupted spiritual leader, Eli. Even though the elder prophet has lost his own way, he gives the young acolyte a gem of wisdom that sets him on a profound and godly trajectory. After Samuel has been wakened several times in the night by God's voice, Eli finally counsels his apprentice, "If someone calls again, say, 'Speak, LORD, your servant is listening'" (v. 9).

The voice of Jesus calls for our repentance and obedience. For courage. For quiet. For us to know how much we are loved.

It's the voice that speaks to an eight-year-old girl's heart.

■■■

Faith for Exiles began with a story about David dropping off his daughter Emily at UC Berkeley, and we promised to give you a glimpse into the process of making that decision.

As I mentioned, I was totally against the idea of my eighteen-year-old attending the school.

But God changed my mind. How?

Over the course of a month or so, our family had at least half a dozen conversations with people I deeply respect that caused me to rethink my assumptions about Berkeley. Well, more to the point, to rethink my assumptions about the value of the school and the active Christian presence in and around it. I began to see the school for what it is: a crazy place, yes, but also an institution that could meet Emily's aspirations for a high-level education *and* a place where her faith could grow.

Those four weeks were unreal. Emily, Jill (her mom, my wife), and I had so many unexpected conversations that slowly shifted our planning. God guided our perceptions through people like Steve, Catherine, Andrew, Kara, Andy, Ryan, Mark, and others. Then one night over dinner, as the decision drew near, we prayed together. I can't explain it, but I experienced a wave of emotion. I powerfully felt that God was showing us that Berkeley was the place. Jesus was calling Emily to the Bay Area and to Cal. He was calling her to be on mission with him there. I still felt some trepidation, but a sense of peace that it was the right choice overwhelmed me.

Now, halfway into her sophomore year, we see how the hand of God was directing her path. She's thriving at the school—and in her faith! About two months after Emily committed to Cal, Jill was diagnosed with brain cancer. It was a horrible year for our family, but having our daughter close was a gift. Her first college choice had been a university on the East Coast, but having Emily in the same time zone was a small part of God's care during a difficult year.

So that's how Emily went to Berkeley: God spoke to us!

Christians from around the planet experience God in their lives. We need to tell these stories of modern-day faith at every turn, from pulpits and in Bible studies but also through social media and in our conversations and every time we think of them.

Jesus speaks.

Following Jesus is more than just believing the right things or feeling warm fuzzies about him. Being Christian is more than being on "team Jesus."

It means we find the very essence of ourselves at his feet.

Experiencing Jesus is entering into a dynamic relationship with him as the author and perfecter of our faith. Experiencing the real Jesus is the starting point and the ending point—the Alpha and the Omega—of resilient faithfulness in digital Babylon.

In a Complex and Anxious Age, Develop the Muscles of Cultural Discernment

Exercising cultural discernment means taking part in a
robust learning community under the authority of the Bible
in order to wisely navigate an accelerated, complex culture.

n the late 1990s, Mark's organization, WisdomWorks, was
given access to experimental artificial intelligence (AI) that
could generate chatbots, computer programs that engage
in text-based conversation. Mark and his team christened the
chatbot WIG, short for Wise Intelligent Guide, and installed it
on their youth website. While each chat was anonymous, with
no identifying information required for teens to interact with
WIG, the ministry team got regular reports on the content of
the chats. It didn't take long for a pattern to emerge.

1. One or two initial goofing-around questions (e.g., What are the names of the seven dwarves?).

2. A test question to make sure the bot was not a person pretending to be a bot (e.g., repeating a question over and over to see if the answers were the same).

3. A warm-up question that posed minimal risk (e.g., What do you think about tattoos? Does God exist?).

4. The actual question the teen wanted to ask, usually about sex, depression, suicide, or abuse (e.g., How do I know if I am gay? What does God think about masturbation? What happens to people who commit suicide? I had sex with my boyfriend; what should I do?).

WIG was basically the ancestor of Google.

■ ■ ■

David has a friend named Seth who is a remarkable guy—an effective leader and just an all-around great human being.

Seth had recently relocated to a new job, and since we hadn't caught up for almost a year, we took an elevator to a rooftop terrace overlooking his newly adopted city where we could talk. He recounted how his kids were doing in the new context.

"We are doing pretty well as a family. We are settling into schools and life here. My teen daughter has taken it hardest. In fact, I recently discovered that her search feed on her phone was filled with YouTube videos about 'How do I know if I am depressed?' and 'How do I deal with anxiety?' I asked her about it, and she said she had found a lot of videos on the issues she was facing."

He paused, looking out over the skyline. "I felt bad she didn't talk to me first. And it made me realize how much mobile phones are giving our kids access to all sorts of ideas about life and how to live it."

Complexity, Stress, and Anxiety

Young people are looking to their devices to make sense of the world around them. As we've pointed out, they are using the screens in their pockets as their counselors, their entertainers, their instructors, and even their sex educators, among many other digital-Sherpa roles. Why make the effort to talk to your parents or teachers when you can privately ask the smartphone in your hand?

The problem we want to identify in this chapter is the challenge of trying to find real, livable wisdom in an accelerated, complex culture. Instantaneous access to information does not equal wisdom. Young people in emerging generations, such as Seth's daughter, are unclear about who to believe and where to turn for input and advice. It's a *good* thing that the internet might provide *some* answers to mental health questions. But is it really the best and deepest and most godly place for finding the *truest* answers?

The undercurrent of all this might be best described as escalating anxiety.

It's now been twenty years since Mark's team first experimented with WIG. AI, algorithms, and machine learning are no longer quirky novelties. They are the hidden gatekeepers to and curators of information and communication "ungoverned by ethical or philosophical norms."[1] They are not anchored to moral and theological norms, either. Instead, math that only a handful of people understand is the cryptic law of the virtual land.

The result? Algorithms tell us how to feel about ourselves and what to think about the world.

As we have said already, and will say again, we are not anti-tech. We are not saying that abundant life and whole-hearted discipleship in exile require a return to landlines or handwritten letters delivered by stagecoach. Our point, rather, is that the disruptive "move fast and break things" ethos of technological innovation is emblematic of digital Babylon's *complexity*—and this often leads to anxiety.

Screens are profoundly changing the human experience and affect us in the following ways:

pushing the tyranny of now

framing and filtering reality

weaponizing humor by making snark cool

overloading our choices

filling our time and distracting our minds

making people even more image conscious

giving people a sense of interacting and participating

Earlier we described digital Babylon as *accelerated* (life moves faster) and *complex* (life is uncertain and difficult to predict). The reaction of many people to these facts of exile is a low-level anxiety that never really goes away and that occasionally ratchets up to high-level anxiety. Three out of five young adults tell us they are "stressed out"; seven out of ten say they are "concerned about the future." And in Barna's first comprehensive study of Gen Z, the generation coming up after

Millennials, anxiety is a recurring theme, especially related to things like education, career, money, and relationships.

Apprehension infiltrates many aspects of modern life. Anxiety about looking your best and eating right. Pressure to perform your best in school and get ahead. Aching questions about calling, jobs, and finances. Frequent comparisons to others on social media. (Gen Z is the most likely generation to admit that seeing others' lives on social media makes them feel insecure about themselves.) Fears about losing faith. Ironic worry about mental health and social wellness. Uncertainty about choosing the right spouse, the right career, the right *anything*, the right *everything*. So many alternatives at our fingertips can be exhausting rather than freeing. We experience paralysis by analysis, overchoice, and complexity.

Take relationships, which have always been a bittersweet domain of human life. In digital Babylon, relationships are more complicated. First, there's social media, which doesn't always (or even usually) make people more social. Second, the road to adulthood, including reaching the typical relational mileposts of marriage and child rearing, is a lot less predictable. Our research shows that young people are delaying marriage in part out of concern they will make the wrong choice in a spouse.

Many are debilitated by worry that their career will take a wrong turn, because there are so many good options to consider. (They're not wrong; it's smart today to prepare for a variety of careers over the course of life, a trend we call "multi-careering.") This generation has been taught to expect and prepare for having it all, so actually making a choice—a choice that necessarily rules out other choices—can feel monumental, and not in a good way. When overwhelmed by all you *could* do, how do you decide what you *should* do without having a nervous breakdown?

In fact, the numbers show this generation is facing unprecedented challenges when it comes to issues of mental health, anxiety, and staying sane and safe. "Hospitals See Growing Numbers of Kids and Teens at Risk for Suicide," reports NPR: "The number of kids who struggle with thoughts of suicide or who attempt to kill themselves is rising. New research . . . finds children ages 5 to 17 visited children's hospitals for suicidal thoughts or attempts about twice as often in 2015 as in 2008."[2]

Life is more complex in digital Babylon. It's not just unlimited access to content. It's the range of ideas and the fact that so many are untethered to orthodox ways of perceiving the world. There is more to think about, more to worry about, more to concern yourself with—and that's just on your Facebook feed on Tuesday morning. Previously unimaginable complexity is creating an epidemic of anxiety in our homes and heads that is ratcheted up in the hearts of the next generation.

What's the solution?

> Cultural discernment, about technology and so much more, is an essential practice of following Jesus in the accelerated, anxiety-producing complexity of digital Babylon.

The second practice of disciple making in digital Babylon is cultural discernment. *In order to live well and wisely in the complexity of digital Babylon—and thereby defuse anxiety—we must build our muscles of cultural discernment:* the ability to compare the beliefs, values, customs, and creations of the world we live in (digital Babylon) to those of the world

Table 3. How Churches Build Cultural Discernment	Prodigals/ Ex-Christians	Nomads/ Unchurched	Habitual Churchgoers	Resilient Disciples
Which of the following, if any, do you regularly experience in your church, parish, or faith community? Please mark any that apply. And if none apply, please feel free to mark that.	✖	◉	🏛	◼
Experiences at Church (% among those who attend)				
Wisdom for how to live faithfully in a secular world.	14%	20%	44%	70%
Wisdom for living with people who believe differently from me.	20%	17%	34%	56%
Help with living wisely when it comes to sex and sexuality.	11%	9%	25%	52%
Help with living wisely when it comes to technology.	8%	7%	20%	50%
Tools for wisely managing my money.	12%	7%	23%	43%

N = 1,514 US 18- to 29-year-olds who grew up as Christians
Source: Barna, February 2018

we belong to (the kingdom of God). And once we've made that comparison, to anchor our lives—including our use of technology—to the theological, moral, and ethical norms of God's kingdom.

Look at the way resilient disciples—our exemplars of effective discipleship among young adults—describe their experiences at church (see table 3). Seven out of ten say they receive "wisdom for how to live faithfully in a secular world." About half say they receive wisdom for living wisely in a pluralistic culture ("people who believe differently from me") and in terms of sex, sexuality, and technology. More than two out of five say their churches provide tools for wisely managing money. In other words, resilient disciples still have room for growth in these areas, but they report far more wisdom-cultivating practices than do habitual churchgoers, nomads, or prodigals who have experience in church.

The evidence is quite clear: how a person thinks and believes makes a huge difference to their resilience. Digital Babylon exerts tremendous influence, but the profile of resilient disciples shows that forming patterns of discernment is one effective way of staying ahead of the curve.

Resilient disciples take part in robust learning communities; that is, they learn how to think in company with other Christians who are learning how to think. This leads to an important conclusion from the research: as exiles in digital Babylon, disciples need a richer, more resilient life of the mind.

Why Cultural Discernment?

In the previous chapter, we indicated that helping people answer the question Who am I, really? is one of the big opportunities open to the church. Another foundational quest for every human is to determine *How should I live? How do I make sense of life? How do I respond well to life's circumstances?* This impulse, this longing, may go unacknowledged, but it won't go away—even in digital Babylon, where colorful, hi-res screens make it easy to ignore.

Many young people (and, let's be honest, older people too) are so dazzled and distracted by their devices that they aren't looking for wisdom. How should I live? hasn't crossed their minds because they're bingeing *Game of Thrones* or *13 Reasons Why* or *Miraculous Ladybug* fan videos, or trading Insta likes, or trying on Snapchat filters, or mainlining free porn straight into their prefrontal cortex.

This is foolishness.

In contrast, listening to wisdom's voice over digital Babylon's 24/7 racket is a top predictor of resilient faith among young adults. For example, we learned that resilients are two and a half times more likely than habitual churchgoers to say they regularly experience "help with living wisely when it comes to technology" in their churches. Why is this so central to following Jesus in exile?

Education by Search Engine

The first reason, as we've been saying, is that the internet has become the primary educator of emerging generations. This has some positives, as any parent who tries to help their high school student understand calculus will tell you. But it also has its downsides. Take, for instance, the cozy relationship this generation has with technology when it comes to sex. Millions of young people are learning about sex—what it is, how to do it, how to think about it—based on what content a search algorithm decides they should encounter online. These encounters happen both intentionally (young people searching for things they'd rather not ask a human being in real life) and unintentionally (young people exposed to pornography and hypersexualized content through mainstream entertainment, social media, and their peers).

Even "good church kids" have a hard time avoiding the complex wonders and wickedness of the wide world. Babylon, in the biblical record and in our culture now, is a leveling force. The allure of bowing down is almost too powerful to resist, even with the help of parental spy software, Christian school covenants, and youth group safety policies.

Way back in the pre-internet olden days, in the 1990s, a great deal of planning and subterfuge was required if a kid wanted to check out porn. What wisdom can older generations offer Millennials and teens who are bombarded with pornographic content whether or not they go looking for it? Porn is more accessible than ever before in human history, and it's taking the sexual imaginations of young men (and, increasingly, young women) captive: a majority of teens believe it is more morally intolerable *not to recycle* than to view pornography.[3]

In digital Babylon, exposure to porn is but one example of something that is not *if* but *when*. We can count on the next generation being exposed to attitudes, values, perspectives, and behaviors antithetical to Christian formation.

How can we pass on deep, potent, lasting Christian faith to young people in an era of moral reversalism, when evil is called good? How can we learn habits that honor God, ourselves, and others with our bodies?

The Tyranny of Now

Porn is not the only potential pitfall in digital Babylon. Help to use tech wisely is also important for discipleship in exile because we are increasingly conditioned to believe that *now* is all that matters. We elevate the latest trend, the newest thing, the hottest take. And the tyranny of now exacerbates the anxiety of modern life.

Personal devices feed the part of our brains that loves instant gratification. They give us a jolt of digital dopamine dozens, if not hundreds, of times a day. We love our memes. Have a funny thought to share with a friend? Hoping you've gotten new Instagram or Facebook likes since the last time you checked? Worried about your grades? Wonder how your stocks are holding up? Digital Babylon invites you to live in the hyperpresent. Whatever your brain is thinking *right now* can appear on a screen near you.

Even some of those credited with creating the tools of digital Babylon are having second thoughts. The most recent book from tech pioneer Jaron Lanier, one of the inventors of virtual reality technology and currently a researcher at Microsoft, is *Ten Arguments for Deleting Your Social Media Accounts Right Now*. In an interview about what is going wrong in the tech sector, he revealed that one of his book's ten arguments is spiritual: "[Social media is] continuous behavior modification on a mass basis, with everyone under surveillance by their devices and receiving calculated stimulus to modify them. . . . It's a bad religion. It's a nerdy, empty, sterile, ugly, useless religion that's based on false ideas."[4]

How can we instill a faith synchronized to the deep time of past, present, and eternal in a now-only world?

Passing the Time

Third, and speaking of time, let's talk about how we spend it. Screens make it possible to cram every idle second with distraction. Birds that are angry. Doodles that jump. Clashing clans. Crushing candy. Zombies versus plants. Friends with words. And we haven't even gotten to the bottomless scroll that is social media.

The two of us travel a lot, and we've noticed a big difference in air travel today compared to ten years ago. No matter how short or long the flight, nearly everyone on the plane is staring at a screen. Sometimes people are working on laptops or tablets. Occasionally, they're reading an ebook. But most of the time, they're using screens to watch entertainment. Or even stranger, when people aren't watching their screens, they leave the flickering pixels flashing in front of them the entire flight. It is disturbingly reminiscent of that scene in Pixar's *Wall-E* of future human beings floating around a spaceship on personal people movers in a permanent state of fixation on the screen hovering just inches from their noses.

Look, watching videos on a plane is a great way to pass the time. But shouldn't the phrase "pass the time" raise at least a tiny red flag? Digital Babylon strip-mines human potential by making it absurdly easy to squander our most precious resource: time!

How can we help exiles consider their discretionary minutes each day—which tally up to their whole lives—as something to be redeemed, not merely passed?

Filtering Reality

Fourth, highly personalized digital environments frame and filter reality so that it's hard to know what's real. If one of the deep questions for human life is *How should I live?* we discover "answers" all the time in the content we consume.

- Sex is for personal fulfillment, and self-denial is unhealthy.
- Any kind of sexual expression is fine, as long as it is consensual.
- Follow your heart.
- Something is true if it feels true.
- If you follow your dreams, you will be happy.
- Marriage is for much later in life, after you're fully developed as a person.

- Family members make fun of one another.
- Workplaces are full of incompetent and dysfunctional people.
- Clergy members are old, irrelevant, and only good for marrying and burying.

The songs we listen to, the shows and movies we watch, the platforms we socialize on, the news we consume—all of these and more create a vision of what is real and how best to respond to that reality. Digital Babylon is constantly telling us, at a very deep, almost unconscious level, what to believe, how to think, what to feel, and how to live.

How can we live in a deeper, truer narrative about ourselves, about our world, about God's nature and his design for flourishing human life?

These are some of the challenges that technology in digital Babylon lays at our door. And as we see in the lives of resilient young Christians, dealing well with them in a community of faith is critical to following Jesus in exile.

The Resilience of Wisdom

Far from being anti-tech, we are anti-foolishness. At the broadest level, the pursuit of wisdom—what we are calling cultural discernment—is the godly answer to rising complexity and its symptom, anxiety. Let's say that again: we can ratchet anxiety down, and ratchet resilience up, by cultivating wisdom. Scripture provides many insights about the role of wisdom in the life of a disciple.

Moreover, exiles use wisdom effectively in their engagement with their times, that is, with the social, spiritual, and political pressures of their context. As you read through this list of biblical characters, think of the complexity and resulting anxiety these exiles must have experienced on their path to faithfulness.

- **Joseph**: He is banished from his family and lives an exilic experience in Egypt. He exercises wisdom in many seasons of his life, from escaping the seductive wife of his boss to helping prepare the nation of Egypt for famine. Joseph's wisdom allows him to live into his calling as civic leader and resource strategist.

- **Jeremiah**: The prophet Jeremiah causes consternation predicting the coming exile for the Jewish people. He also writes beautifully and persuasively about the role of discernment to those experiencing exile. He advises exiles to make a fruitful life (plant trees, build homes, marry and have children), to bless those around them in every way possible, and to seek God's best, especially through prayer, for the people they live among (see Jer. 29). Resilience is at the heart of his admonition. Jeremiah's insights about living faithfully in exile seem to have provided a road map for a young Daniel (in Daniel 9 we see him reading the scroll written by Jeremiah) and echo still today.

- **Daniel**: This exemplar exile demonstrates wisdom in his negotiation with his captors over diet; he learns the language of Babylon, including taking on the name of a Babylonian god; he advocates for the lives of pagan philosophers; he interprets the dream of the volatile king, at great risk to himself; he serves three different political regimes as a court advisor; he studies Scripture for insights about life in exile; and despite his social status later in life, he's willing to trade everything to follow God. Daniel's effective use of wisdom allows him to serve Yahweh as an orator, diplomat, and statesman.

- **Shadrach, Meshach, and Abednego**: The story of the courageous three exiles is narrated by Daniel, and among their displays of wisdom is, of course, their courage not to bow down to the Babylonian idol. What is remarkable about their story is their response to coercion: our God is powerful enough to save us from the fiery furnace; *but even if he doesn't*, we're not going to bow down (see Dan. 3:17–18). Their wisdom shows us today how to reject the idols of our age.

- **Esther**: This exile demonstrates wisdom first by listening to the counsel of her elders (Mordecai) and then by acting with faith—even while feeling a bit fatalistic ("If I must die, I must die" [Esther 4:16])—to save her people. Esther wisely uses her influence, which is at least partly a function of her surpassing beauty, to effect social change for the Jewish people.

- **Mordecai**: A critical supporting actor in Esther's story, Mordecai sees the power plays happening in the society around him and provides an effective call to action for Esther: "Who knows if perhaps you were made queen for just such a time as this?" (Esther 4:14). He shows what it means to exercise cultural discernment and call the younger generation to the lives of purpose they were meant to live.

- **Peter**: This apostle writes to his fellow believers and encourages them to think of themselves as "sojourners" in a foreign society. He reminds Christ followers of their history of exile and what it means to be holy. Peter's letters remind us that even those of us under the new covenant can think about faithfulness in light of being an exilic community.

- **John**: While in exile on the isle of Patmos, John writes down the revelation he receives, which includes a vision of the seven churches of Asia Minor. He reminds them to exercise discernment as a community of believers. If you read the things the Spirit reveals to John about each of the seven churches, you can see how important it is for every local church to think about and develop the muscles of discernment. Even the very nature of John's repeated refrain—"Anyone with ears to hear must listen to the Spirit and understand what he is saying to the churches"—is a type of wisdom-seeking imperative.

As you review these exile stories, what do you notice? We think one of the most powerful themes is the power of discernment for producing *faithfulness*. We can draw inspiration by studying these scriptural examples of exiles who put wisdom into practice. Simply put, we can't live in times of complexity without wisdom, the human capacity to understand life from God's perspective—or, to put it another way, a practical understanding of how to live as God designed us.

In a complex and anxious age, we need to develop the muscles of wisdom and discernment. Like a good workout, the pressures of following Jesus in our current environment force us to get stronger—or else suffer the consequences. If we don't put in the effort to swim upstream, our faith is going to wash out.[5] In light of the coercive powers of our present age, resilience looks like developing what Jesus prays for us to be—in the world but not of the world.

In but not of.

We see this yearning in resilient disciples in their identification with the statement "I want to find a way to follow Jesus that connects with the world I live in" (87 percent say this is *completely* or *mostly true* of me). Resilient young Christians desire to connect their faith in Jesus with the world they inhabit. They don't want their *spiritual* lives and their *real* lives to be separate things. They expect their faith to have a transforming impact on the world.

Exercising this kind of cultural engagement seems to make for better life outcomes. Correlation is not causation, but from our experience, it's no coincidence that resilient disciples are much less likely than others to describe themselves as "stressed out." Forty-four percent report feeling stressed, compared to half of habitual churchgoers (52 percent) and two-thirds of nomads (68 percent) and prodigals (64 percent). Resilients are likewise less likely than others to say they are "concerned about the future."

So how do we turn these kinds of insights into action? Here are three starting points on the way to wisdom.

Don't Hide under a Rock

One of the first principles we see in the lives of biblical exiles is that they don't bury their heads in the sand. The same must be true of us today. We must develop the right mind-set of cultural engagement, the right posture. In digital Babylon, the question is not if but when—not *if* we will face doubts, questions, content, images, ideas, and worldviews that are antithetical to Christian faith but *when*. It's better to face what's coming. We must not hide under a rock.

We can't simply shelter the next generation (or ourselves) and hope they don't come into contact with the worst the

85

world has to offer. We have to expect it. We have to prepare for it. We must carefully and intentionally develop a resilience that is in but not of the world. Making resilient disciples does not mean *protecting* young Christians but *preparing* them for life on mission.

Resilient disciples already embrace this mind-set. They want their lives to reflect Jesus in all they do. They expect their Sundays to invade their weekdays. They perceive Jesus to be at work outside the walls of the church.

Here are some of the questions we contemplate when we have the right mind-set:

- Do I understand my relationship as a Christian to culture?
- Do I know how to reflect on and respond to culture?
- Do I understand my identity apart from culture?
- Am I driven by fear of culture or the world?
- Do I see how Jesus enters into culture to meet people?
- Do I understand my role in representing Jesus in my context?

Here's how this mind-set might affect a huge problem: porn. Some try to ignore it, but those with wisdom won't. For the first time in human history, explicit sexual images are floating through the air and available at the swipe of a finger. We can't avoid the topic, and we can't have just one conversation.

We can try to protect young Christians, and that's a good step up from ignoring the problem. Setting solid expectations about screen use and monitoring Wi-Fi and cellular data are important. But just trying to close down access to porn isn't sufficient.

What if we tried to help the next generation (and ourselves) think missionally about the problem? What if we prepared them to have a different mind-set and a different way of thinking and talking about the problem? We find in our research that most teens today think porn is positive or neutral. Few think it's a bad thing. What if we taught our kids why porn is corrosive to our character and our souls, as well as to our families and coworkers, from a *missional* point of view? What if we helped them become capable of having helpful, healthy conversations with their peers, who are most likely to think porn is no big deal?

In our conversations with our kids, our talks about porn go something like this: "It's very hard to grow up today because of online porn. And I am really sorry. Screens make it tougher than ever to keep our hearts and minds pure, but we can find grace and forgiveness in Jesus when we mess up and repent. Let's also think about how you can help your friends—to represent the truth and grace of Jesus—because it's very likely they struggle with this."

Having the right mind-set helps us become resilient by helping us properly understand our priorities as Christians: we are on mission with Jesus, even in exile.

Anchor to the Bible

David's family sometimes reads the book of Ecclesiastes at dinner. The Kinnamans are a family of achievers, and it's good to be reminded of the vanity of self-driven, self-regulated effort. (Daughter Annika once reminded her basketball teammates that chasing stats on the court is no better than chasing the wind.)

We have both found ourselves wondering why churches don't teach the Bible's Wisdom Literature more often (Proverbs,

Lamentations, Song of Songs, Ecclesiastes), because this genre speaks so powerfully to the temptations of digital Babylon (ambition, sex, anxiety, and trauma).

A second insight we see in the biblical model of exiles is their submission to what God is telling them, especially through the Scriptures. They view God as living and active, desiring that his people seek his direction. As we noted above, Daniel reports that he was "reading the word of the LORD, as revealed to Jeremiah the prophet" (Dan. 9:2).

As Christians today, we too should aim to be an exilic community that seeks God's direction under the authority of Scripture. This dovetails with the themes we discussed in the previous chapter—that we should orient ourselves toward the voice of Jesus in our lives. How? We acknowledge that the Bible is our authoritative source for wisdom. And wisdom is held up as a worthy but rarely traveled path.

Our research shows that resilient disciples hold a range of Bible-centered perceptions and practices far more than their Christian peers (see table 4). Reading the Bible makes them feel closer to God. Bible teaching at their churches is relevant and increases their love for the Bible. In short, the lived reality of resilients is that the Bible is authoritative and central to their faith.

Anchoring to the Bible helps us weather the ups, downs, and sideways of exile.

Don't Just Engage; Prepare to Engage

A third pattern of biblical exiles is periods of preparation leading up to more public engagement with society. We can't live life *on* mission if we haven't been prepared *for* mission. The stories of Daniel, Joseph, and Esther show the importance

Table 4. What Builds Resilient Disciples? Anchoring to the Bible	Prodigals/ Ex-Christians	Nomads/ Unchurched	Habitual Churchgoers	Resilient Disciples
Percentage who strongly agree with each statement				
The Bible is the inspired Word of God and contains truth about the world.*	8%	29%	49%	100%
Reading the Bible makes me feel closer to God.	10%	21%	44%	87%
The Bible teaching I receive in my church is relevant to my life.	8%	15%	45%	86%
At church I get wisdom for how the Bible applies to my life.	15%	26%	52%	86%
At church I gain greater love for the Bible.	17%	21%	47%	85%
The Bible is the foundation of all teaching at my church.	11%	29%	49%	83%
The Bible contains everything I need to know to live a meaningful life.	7%	17%	39%	74%
The Bible is totally accurate in all of the principles it teaches.	8%	18%	41%	76%

N = 1,514 US 18- to 29-year-olds who grew up as Christians
Source: Barna, February 2018
*This statement was used in part to define resilient disciples.

of preparation. In fact, many biblical stories, including those of Abraham, Moses, Samuel, David, and Jesus, demonstrate this clear principle: God uses early experiences to shape the hearts and minds of his servants. There is no such thing as a wasted moment. David demonstrates this beautifully when he says that his death matches with lions and bears have given him confidence that God will help him defeat Goliath (1 Sam. 17:34–37). His preparation leads to faithful engagement.

This is especially true in the biblical record of Daniel. The entire first chapter of his story is a revelation on the importance of early years in shaping an in-but-not-of way of life in exile. Daniel's story seems to demonstrate important faith formation at work *before* he's taken into exile and also *during* his time in exile. He's learning the language and customs of Babylon; he's engaging his peers and mentors—people who don't believe what he does—and learning to be faithful, not just in spite of but in the midst of incredible pressures.

Fast-forward to the present. Our research among resilient disciples shows that churches can meaningfully help to build cultural discernment in the lives of young people, but doing so is not easy. (Consider table 3 again.) A strong majority of resilients say their churches help them build wisdom for how to live faithfully in a secular world (70 percent), but the percentage drops off substantially when it comes to more specific topics. About half indicate that their churches aid their wisdom for living with people who believe differently (56 percent), help with living wisely when it comes to sex and sexuality (52 percent), and guide them when it comes to living wisely with technology (50 percent). Nearly half say their churches provide tools for wisely managing money (43 percent). (This is important because the Bible makes a big deal about faithful stewardship of finances, and teens in Gen Z, especially, are strongly motivated by financial attainment.)

One of the strongest predictors of being a resilient exile is saying that their church helps them live wisely when it comes to technology. This is still something many resilients need help with, but when it happens, it has a powerful effect.

In some ways, the church is not preparing young disciples for the world as it is. Cultural discernment is about teaching them not just what to think but also how to live. We must prepare them for the world as it truly is, not as we wish it to be. Exiles in the Bible are a good reminder that God finds leaders, prophets, and change makers in order to help lead his people during times of upheaval. In ancient times and today, exiles change our "how" thinking and reorient our "why"—they help people find faithfulness in a strange land so that the witness to God can intersect with the world as it is.

Here's an example. Daniel advocated for the lives of his philosophical and spiritual adversaries. As recorded in Daniel 2, Daniel tells the commander of the king's guard, who is trying to pacify the raving-mad king, not to kill the pagan philosophers and wise men of Babylon. Instead, Daniel risks his very life to enter the king's throne room and attempt the impossible: interpret the man's dream. This is an example of changing "how" and "why": Daniel shows how to express empathy and solidarity with people who are our enemies, because that's the experience of living faithfully with others within a pluralistic society.

Our friend Jim Henderson told us recently about a young man who works on his production team. The young man is more theologically and socially conservative than Jim himself, but, as Jim reports, "I'm honored he's willing to work with a seventy-year-old guy. He is creative, opinionated, and thoughtful, and we talk openly about our differences. As a mentor, I want him to become comfortable engaging with people who hold vastly different opinions." Jim is helping his team member prepare to engage—and that will help him become resilient.

Becoming a Learning Community

Mark remembers seeing the course list for his daughter Skye as she was registering for fashion design school in New York City. Most classes had titles like "Space and Materiality," "Sustainable Systems," and "Time." But the course that caught his attention was called "Fake." It was a seminar and a studio in which students made things based on the content from the course. His first thought was, *What exactly am I paying for here?* But his conversations with Skye over the duration of the semester were most frequently about this class.

In the class, students were assigned the task of creating fake memories and posting them alongside real memories to see if their classmates could determine real from fake. It was interesting to Skye to see fellow students thinking and reflecting, shaping the way they discern the world. When you stop to think about it, if you are going into a creative field, when does something you create become real? Is it possible to make something that is, in fact, fake? In fashion, a designer can make something that is considered real, while a knockoff made of nearly identical materials is a fake. Why?

As you can imagine, it didn't take long for someone in the class to bring up the topic of an experience with God. How does one know whether it is real or fake? That set of questions led Skye and her classmates to some memorable conversations.

What if we did these kinds of exercises in our churches and families? What if we gave young people the tools and the language to discern between concepts such as real and fake—and so much more? Doing so would be useful in helping them learn to act with wisdom. If this is the kind of training young artists receive, we ought to use the same rigor to develop disciplines of cultural discernment for exiles navigating between their faith and the culture.

To do so, however, will require some major changes in the way we think about learning.

Learning in Digital Babylon

Digital Babylon is a radically new environment, and it requires a commitment to learning, to the search for truth and beauty, in brand-new ways. Having studied this topic for a decade and spoken to hundreds of thousands of teens, we firmly believe this:

> To instill and transmit cultural discernment in digital Babylon, faith communities and households must become robust learning communities.

This is not just about training smart or gifted kids, although they are certainly important (and often ignored by ministry efforts). Instead, this is about training all young people, of all capabilities and callings, to learn, to think, to understand, to comprehend, to act.

We need to teach critical thinking, how to evaluate and understand propaganda, fake and real, truth and post-truth, worldview and theology, and so much more. We should offer classes and courses and seminars on all sorts of topics—tailored to the pressures and questions young Christians are actually experiencing. We should buy young people books and send them links to helpful videos and be prepared to discuss good content. We must expose them to ideas and concepts from people with different skin colors and genders. (We should do this not only because we find it so easy to assume that "people like me" must be right but also because Gen Z and Millennials have come to expect diversity—rightly so—and believe they have much to learn from people different from themselves.)

We once heard historian Molly Worthen talk about the importance of teaching young people about their own theological traditions. In our research among resilient disciples, we found evidence of this (mostly untapped) appetite. Exposing young disciples to a greater range of information and insight about where they come from is one crucial aspect of forming a coherent identity.

This may sound like really hard work. That's because it is! But what could be more important? We absolutely must expose them to the deep, rigorous thinking of other Christians, especially those in careers and areas of study they care about.

Brett McCracken, a friend of David's, and his wife, Kira, took six twentysomethings to Europe a few years back. "It was part discipleship, part church history, part ministry to churches in different parts of England. We saw so much growth in these young people during this time and in the years that followed." European mission trips may not be accessible to all, but taking time to invest relationally, intellectually, *and* historically can help the young grow in faith.

Brett also hosts movie screenings at his house with young adults from church. They view the movie together, then discuss it afterward, exploring both the artistic merits and the theological themes. Brett says, "Young adults are eager to 'go deep' in talking about a movie and exploring the theological issues raised in films."

Learning in Action

Our research supports the contention that learning matters. Young resilient disciples report nearly double the spiritual intake in a typical year compared to habitual churchgoers and about six times the number of hours of Christian content compared to nomads and prodigals. Over the course of years, this adds up. The habits of learning, of steeping ourselves in a Christian way of thinking and seeing the world, matter.

We also found evidence that resilients experience less overall screen time than other segments of young Christians and former Christians. It's still a lot of screen time, but it's less compared to their peers. This fact, along with their increased hours of participating in Christian events and taking in Christian content, is strong ballast against the unpredictable waves of digital Babylon. Their cultural discernment muscles are getting a better workout.

How can we commit ourselves to putting in more time together to learn, to pursue knowledge and beauty, in our current context? How can we meaningfully increase the number of hours we devote to following our Lord in these trying and confusing times?

We must commit ourselves to higher quality and quantity of hours devoted to the life of discipleship.

The Learning Reformation

A reformation of learning is already under way all around us, and it represents an incredible opportunity for the church as we think about raising disciples in digital Babylon. Here are some of the factors combining to fire the reformation.

First, God wired human beings to learn. The basic impulses for the learning revolution are hardwired into our DNA. We want to grow. We aspire to gain new skills and perspectives.

Second, in the larger context for learning in today's digital commons, people can learn what they want, when they want,

Habits Matter: Resilient Disciples Digest Nearly Double the Hours of Christian Content Annually

Annual Intake of Faith Content, Fifteen- to Twenty-Three-Year-Olds

Prodigals /
Ex-Christians

Nomads /
Unchurched

Habitual
Churchgoers

Resilient
Disciples

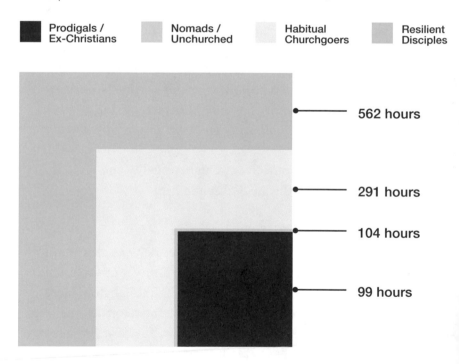

562 hours

291 hours

104 hours

99 hours

at a price they want (usually for free), and how they want (thanks, YouTube). Much of what passes for learning is actually just infotainment. But at the same time, there has never been a better time in human history to learn something. We can access free learning content on sites such as Khan Academy. We can take master classes online. We can earn a degree through online programs. All of this is on top of other traditional, nondigital learning opportunities.

Third, most young Christians want to learn. In one recent study, we discovered that millions of practicing Christians want to learn in all sorts of ways—sometimes for personal enrichment, sometimes for a degree program. David recently met Megan, a mother of young kids, who is attending seminary "because I want to be better prepared to help my kids navigate theology and today's culture." How cool is that?

The idea that we need a new approach to learning is something researchers at Barna have been seeing since our work on *You Lost Me*. Our pedagogical structures assume that the bigger the youth group, the bigger the church, the more learning that's happening—because, I mean, *look at all those people*! But the things one can learn in a large group setting, for all its merits, are different from what one can learn in a smaller classroom or living room.

So what is the solution to this dilemma?

Preach, but Don't Only Preach

Effective preaching is as important as ever, but it's not sufficient for bringing about whole-life transformation. What do we mean?

Churches play a foundational role in forming a culturally discerning mind-set among resilient disciples. All of the evidence points to the fact that sermons are an important part of that equation. However, the data also indicates that an hour (or less) a week—or, more likely, an hour or so every few weeks, when a young Christian shows up for church—is simply not a sufficient amount of "weight" to tone a heart bloated with hundreds of hours of content from digital Babylon.

Churches need more than good sermons to disciple in digital Babylon; we also need other structures of learning: courses, programs, mentoring, field-based experiences, mission trips, and more.

Take, for example, the subject of human sexuality and a theology of the body. Even if we were to hear an incredible sermon series—and we must have deep, thoughtful, biblical sermons on this subject—that handful of sermons couldn't possibly be enough to adequately engage the depth, texture, and richness of Christian teaching on this topic. We need something like Human Sexuality 101 and 201 courses, ways to engage thoughtful, smart, connected, curious, and cynical minds with sturdy Christian content.

And while we're at it, let's talk about the mantras we ministry leaders repeat to ourselves about *effectiveness*. This is mostly about the size of the crowd or the rave reviews we get for our teaching series. The two of us have actually heard comments like, "It's a sin to bore a young person at church." This is well-meaning, of course; we get the heart behind statements like this. But the idea is wrong. Sometimes teaching rich, robust truths is, let's admit it, hard work and can lead to boredom in an age of short attention spans. But in our efforts to keep things from becoming boring, we've put the cookies on the bottom shelf for the next generation. We've oversimplified things. We give Brand Jesus pep talks that inspire in the moment but melt into the digital ether as soon as young people walk out of church. This is the problem with entertaining-but-shallow Christian experiences for youth and young adults. What's worse, young people who are *ready* to grow, who *want* to push past the boredom, are disappointed. This is how we end up losing some of the brightest young minds and talents, particularly creatives, entrepreneurs, and science-minded students.

We have to do better. Good preaching alone won't cut it.

Teach the Whole Gospel

We define the whole gospel, based on thinking from many others, as a four-chapter Christian story: creation-fall-redemption-restoration. In too many places, we teach an abbreviated and insufficient two-part story: fall and redemption. You are a sinner and you need Jesus.

Those two elements are the truth of the human condition and the center of the gospel. But to be whole, they need to be set in the context of the opening chapter (God created human beings in his image, with desire and potential for goodness, truth, and beauty) and understood in light of the closing chapter (God's ultimate plan for the world is to set things right and renew all things).

Most resilient disciples embrace these four elements, though their belief in the fall sags. Only 60 percent strongly agree with the idea that "all human beings are essentially broken and flawed because they have rebelled against God" (see table 5).

The point is that we should be regularly involved in clearly, compellingly conveying the entire scope of God's truth about the world in both sermons and other learning structures. Only the fullness of God's story can help young disciples make sense of their world in exile.

Table 5. The Gospel in Four Chapters: Creation-Fall-Redemption-Restoration	Prodigals/ Ex-Christians	Nomads/ Unchurched	Habitual Churchgoers	Resilient Disciples
Percentage who strongly agree with each statement	✖	◉	⛪	▌
God created humans in his image, with desire and potential for goodness, truth, and beauty.	22%	49%	62%	91%
All human beings are essentially broken and flawed because they have rebelled against God.	8%	16%	32%	60%
I believe that Jesus Christ was crucified and raised from the dead to conquer sin and death.*	12%	43%	56%	100%
God's ultimate plan for the world is to set things right and to renew all things.	15%	33%	43%	78%

N = 1,514 US 18- to 29-year-olds who grew up as Christians
Source: Barna, February 2018
*This statement was used in part to define resilient disciples.

Experiment with Learning and Thinking Structures

No matter how we slice it, we consistently find that the next generation of Christians lacks sufficient thinking structures to engage the world. For example, we found that only 4 percent—just one out of every twenty-five teenagers today—has what we might call a biblical worldview. This points to the need for deeper patterns of faith engagement, more and better ways of teaching and learning.

As Gabe Lyons and David wrote about in *Good Faith*, this could include preparing young people to ask and answer four questions: What's right? What's wrong? What's missing? What's confused? Giving young people tools to address these four questions allows them a wider range of biblical—in-but-not-of—responses to their world. Things that are "right" should be celebrated. We should identify "wrong" things and fix them, or find a better way. "Missing" things should be found or created. And "confused" elements of our culture should be clarified. These simple questions can help us exiles engage our world more faithfully.

This might look like what our friends Brooke and Christian do. They spend at least thirty minutes during mealtime after church each week talking with their young kids about what they learned and experienced in church and how it connects to their world. We can imagine a web-based platform of videos, readings, and assessments that help young people discover God-shaped truth about their calling. We can picture a church creating comprehensive courses on topics that matter to adolescents and young adults. We can envision a group of Christians in our city creating a "seminary program" for high schoolers, asking them to learn rich theological truths that they can apply throughout the rest of their lives.

We believe the church can and will rise to the learning reformation that is under way. We need to return to our historic roots and build up the muscles of young Christians. We need to encourage young people to read more, watch more, learn more—content suffused with a Christian understanding of the world. We must become and be a part of a robust learning community if we are to thrive as exiles in digital Babylon.

We see green shoots of learning sprouting up all over the place. We just have to water this budding movement!

■ ■ ■

One night at the dinner table, the Kinnaman family was talking about cynicism in entertainment and cynical characters in movies and shows we had seen.

My teenage daughter Annika brought up *Good Luck Charlie*, a fun and humorous show that aired for seven seasons on the Disney Channel. We all agreed that one of the characters, Gabe, was the most cynical person in the fictional family.

"You know, I remember trying to be like Gabe sometimes," Anni exclaimed as she noticed the blurry line between screens and real life. "I tried to make jokes like the family on *Good Luck Charlie*. Like Gabe. And it was weird because I totally remember that no one in our *real* family laughed. And when I said those things out loud, they didn't really seem very funny. They just seemed kind of mean."

"Anni, that's so observant!" I cheered. "I'm so proud of you for thinking it through and noticing that. The more we use wisdom in what we watch and how it affects us, the more we can live differently, like Jesus wants us to."

Qoheleth's Discernment Method

Here's a thinking structure devised by Mark that you can experiment with in your household or ministry group.

For churches and families sorely in need of wisdom, Ecclesiastes is an underleveraged book of the Bible. The writer identifies himself as Qoheleth, the one who assembles or gathers. This could be understood in a number of ways. One who assembles and gathers people. One who assembles and gathers wisdom and insight. I (Mark) describe Qoheleth as *one who searches*. Given that a search engine is used more times in a day than a fork, this interpretation makes sense for our times.

Ecclesiastes is a unique book because Qoheleth's musings are derived from his observations about nature, people, society, culture, and work. He is learning directly about life—and indirectly about God—by observing life apart from God, or life "under the sun."

In the early days of the internet, my ministry engaged students on the internet to help them on their journey of discipleship. Our team did movie and music reviews to help young people navigate popular culture. But as the volume of media and various channels increased, we just couldn't cover everything. The movie reviewers couldn't keep up with every movie coming out—neither could the organization's budget! All the content "under the sun" just kept multiplying.

Realizing it was impossible to filter all media streaming across the screens of the next generation to help them make decisions in advance about what media to consume, I decided the best we could do was teach them to discern culture on their own as they encountered it in real time. Based on Qoheleth's grand experiment of observing God indirectly, I derived some basic questions for wisely discerning media. (My kids, rolling their eyes after every movie or TV show they watched together, learned to discern culture like this. You're welcome, Matlock kids! Don't mention it.)

Where Is God? Who Is God?

While watching reruns of *The Brady Bunch* with my kids, I asked, "Where is God in this story?" All of a sudden, we realized this was a family without a relationship with Christ. We didn't see them pray. We never saw them consult the Scriptures to find wisdom for their problems. We did, however, sometimes see biblical principles at play in the Brady family's adventures. When a football hit Marcia in the face, one of my kids remarked that sometimes God allows things to happen in our lives that seem bad to help us grow. Not bad for an elementary schooler! Christians do something similar when we read the book of Esther, an exile herself. God is not mentioned anywhere in its pages, yet we see him actively moving throughout her story.

It's comparatively easy to find God through his direct revelation in Scripture and in our relationship with Christ, but seeing God *indirectly* requires intentionality. Cultural discernment, much like wisdom, begins with God.

It's possible for a creator to write God out of the picture entirely, and helping young minds consider this possibility can be very powerful all on its own. It's great to discover God in an unlikely place, but it's also worth noticing when God isn't an active part of a human-created universe.

But noticing where God is missing is not enough. If a person living in exile is to discern culture well, they must also get to know God's true character. There are many human creations of art and story that include a portrayal of God that is false or misleading. An image of God that is weak, unloving, distant, or cruel needs to be identified and then corrected.

Daniel and his friends were able to navigate a culture distant from the ways of God because they knew who God truly is. When Shadrach, Meshach, and Abednego stood tall instead of bowing before Nebuchadnezzar's golden idol, what they knew about God gave them the courage to make that choice. They knew he is mighty. They knew he has promised to protect his people. But they also knew it was possible he would not save them because his ways are above human understanding.

A generation of exiles with a limited understanding of God is prone to bowing, and so it's not enough only to ask *where* God is. We must also ask *who* God is and help them find out for themselves.

What Claim Is Being Made about How Life Works?

Every human creation declares something about how the world works, and identifying that worldview is an important part of cultural discernment. Whether we're dealing with great works of literature, the latest horror movie, or a James Bond film, the author has a worldview. James Bond movies portray one idea of masculinity. What is true or not true about that idea? What about Bond's notions of survival or good and evil?

It's important to recognize how often art gets life right. Sometimes artists are more in touch with the human condition than many of us in ministry! The artist's claim about how life works is often what draws people to their art, and talking about the worldview underlying their creation is a great way to help young people understand their own claims about life.

Here are a couple follow-ups to move us from reflection toward synthesis: How do these claims compare to God's path for human thriving? How would this creation be different if Jesus's way were followed?

Where Can Hope and Redemption Be Found— If at All?

Qoheleth looked around and saw nothing but meaninglessness under the sun. Working humbly and enjoying people before you die are better than total emptiness, but those pursuits, too, are ultimately meaningless. Most media today come to similar conclusions. But Qoheleth found something more "above the sun," and that is often the missing component in today's stories. (Read Eccles. 12:1–7.)

Every character is placing hope in something, but what? Do they find redemption, or does their hope fail them? What is the source of power for their transformation?

Even as followers of Christ, we sometimes try to manage sin in our own strength, feeding the law of the flesh inside us rather than trusting in the grace of Jesus. If we who know Christ struggle with where to find hope and redemption, it's no wonder that secular expressions of these things are skewed as well.

Here's a follow-up to move us from reflection toward synthesis: How does this song, story, or work of art change when hope and redemption are found in Jesus?

The practice of answering Qoheleth's questions can build resilience in our lives as we interpret the world around us, for it isn't only the creative work of humans that an exile has to discern but also current events and daily interactions. Paul encouraged the Corinthians to "take captive every thought to make it obedient to Christ" (2 Cor. 10:5 NIV), and we think this is the kind of cultural critical thinking he would have in mind for us today.

When Isolation and Mistrust Are the Norms, Forge Meaningful, Intergenerational Relationships

Building meaningful relationships means being devoted to fellow believers we want to be around and become.

My wife, Jade, and I (Mark) are sitting across the living room from a young couple. Their wedding is coming up, and I have been asked to officiate. Even though this twosome is younger than usual, especially with the trend of Millennials getting married in their late twenties, my first session with them leaves me feeling impressed. They display maturity beyond their years and have all the building blocks of a strong relationship that normally lead to a healthy marriage.

As I always do, I've asked them to do a premarital inventory before the wedding; this can help set up a couple for communication success in the early months and years of marriage. After some discussion, it becomes obvious that neither has much interest in church even though they both grew up as Christians. Realizing the delicate nature of the subject, I gently venture in, asking about their spiritual backstories.

The mood in the room changes. After an awkward moment, they turn to each other, each hoping the other will jump in first. Finally, the bride-to-be shifts in her seat and begins. "We haven't talked about church and that stuff a lot. It's something we both *may* want to do, but it isn't really *that* important to us. Besides, it just feels like a show every weekend, you know? It's just like spiritual entertainment."

"Yeah, what she said," says the young man, and he mumbles some additional details about his parents and about not being against "any of that stuff."

I can sense both are uncomfortable, and since these are the first hours of our friendship, I decide not to press further until more trust has been built.

Fast-forward two weeks.

The next session comes along. I open the folder to review the assessment results with the smiling twentysomethings and to discuss areas in their relationship in which they have strong compatibility and areas in which they'll have some work to do. I glance at the printout of results. It shows that faith and spirituality are an opportunity for them to grow as a couple; in fact, these areas also represent the least agreement between the otherwise stable pair.

"This part of your marriage, if addressed, could lead to some of the greatest breakthroughs in your intimacy as a couple and offer strength and hope in times of crisis," I say as I begin to read the insights from the assessment.

Quite suddenly, just like the first time, the mood in the room turns. The bride-to-be starts talking over me as if she is having a conversation with someone who isn't in the room. She is speaking softly and quietly, her head turned away. I try to reel the connection back in, but the young woman continues to talk, her attention directed elsewhere. This goes on for nearly five minutes. It's as though she doesn't like the radio station she is listening to, so she creates her own stream of content.

Finally, I lean back in my seat.

And then, as if nothing had happened, the bride-to-be looks at me and asks with a smile, "What's next?"

I feel a sinking feeling in my gut. What did the church do that would create this kind of avoidance behavior? What happened to this poor church girl that she could be so deeply wounded?

■■■

This young woman is an extreme example, but we often see a less severe but similar reaction among other young Christians. It's often rooted in strong emotions.

pain
disconnection
emotional distance
skepticism
withdrawal

Consider that this younger generation has grown up in the most corporate (in the business sense) expression of the local church since its inception. Its leaders have often acted more like entrepreneurs and showmen than prophets and shepherds. Meanwhile, churches have lost influence in their local communities.[1] This generation is the first to form their identities—and their perceptions of church—amid high-profile sexual abuse scandals and sky-high levels of church skepticism.

At the same time that the church is fighting back perceptions of irrelevance and extremism, social pressure is leading to more isolation. All of this means that young people have to travel a long road in order to find supportive relationships, inside or outside the church. This leads us to the third practice of resilient disciple making in digital Babylon: *when isolation and mistrust are the norms, forge meaningful, intergenerational relationships.*

Resilient disciples' connections in the church are far and away more extensive than those of habitual churchgoers, nomads, or prodigals. The vast majority of resilients firmly assert that "the church is a place where I feel I belong" and "I am connected to a community of Christians" (see table 6). Fewer than half of habituals experience this kind of relational connectedness. Furthermore, as we'll see, the emotions resilients feel in their churches are far warmer and more positive than others experience. Their churches feel like a family and are made up of people they actually want to be around and become.

Resilients tend to maintain a rich set of friendships and relational connections; they are *people* people. They exhibit exactly the kind of profile we would hope to see in our own lives and in the lives of those we care about. And this is the case not just because they shake hands with other Christians on their way out the church door on Sundays. Something deeper is going on relationally.

Table 6. **What Builds Resilient Disciples? Meaningful Relationships**	Prodigals/ Ex-Christians	Nomads/ Unchurched	Habitual Churchgoers	Resilient Disciples
Percentage who strongly agree with each statement	✖	◉	⛪	📖
The church is a place where I feel I belong.	5%	10%	43%	88%
There is someone in my life who encourages me to grow spiritually.	23%	31%	50%	85%
I am connected to a community of Christians.	7%	7%	33%	82%
When growing up, I had close personal friends who were adults from my church, parish, or faith community.	27%	31%	53%	77%
I admire the faith of my parents.	16%	29%	45%	72%
I feel emotionally close to someone at my church.	5%	6%	30%	64%

N = 1,514 US 18- to 29-year-olds who grew up as Christians
Source: Barna, February 2018

There are two signposts that can lead the way toward meaningful, intergenerational relationships; one is aspirational and the other is reality-based.

The aspirational element is best attained by keeping in mind what the church represents: "the best example of what God can do with human community."[2] Throughout Scripture, and especially in the New Testament, we read exhortations about this kind of Spirit-transformed, cross-shaped community of believers.

I appeal to you, brothers and sisters, in the name of our Lord Jesus Christ, that all of you agree with one another in what you say and that there be no divisions among you, but that you be perfectly united in mind and thought. (1 Cor. 1:10 NIV)

And we urge you, brothers and sisters, warn those who are idle and disruptive, encourage the disheartened, help the weak, be patient with everyone. (1 Thess. 5:14 NIV)

Bear with each other and forgive one another if any of you has a grievance against someone. Forgive as the Lord forgave you. (Col. 3:13 NIV)

What a compelling, beautiful picture of the potential of human community!

While we keep this high calling of Christian community in mind, we must also balance it with an "earthy, everyday" understanding of Christian relationships.[3] High, heavenly aspiration is kept in tension with the lived reality. In other words, relationships are never perfect.

Dietrich Bonhoeffer reminds us in his seminal book *Life Together* that we don't merely bear one another's burdens; the true burden is *bearing one another*. We overlook offense. We forgive. We show mercy and grace. We disabuse ourselves of our own pipe dreams and illusions of Christian community in order for the power of that community to take effect.[4]

Living in the tension between these—the great good of Christian community and the lived reality of its imperfections—is hard, soul-crafting work. And because of the ascendant cultural forces of isolation and loneliness, this work is more needed than ever.

Isolation Nation

We experience some of our highest highs and lowest lows in the context of relationships. Any perusal of literature or history demonstrates the fundamental relational brokenness of human beings.

Fast-forward to today, and relationships are no easier. Despite the progress made in the fields of counseling, psychology, and psychiatry, staying on the path to relational wholeness continues to require grinding effort. On this side of heaven, we'll never truly experience relational wholeness due to the inherent fractures endemic to human hearts.

Digital Babylon doesn't make things any easier, even though we are more technologically connected. We have more tools of communication at our disposal than ever before, and there are truly wonderful elements to life in the modern world. Who would want to go back to the 1990s, when we had only landlines and snail mail and we couldn't FaceTime to check in with relatives or friends who lived abroad?

Yet in spite of all the technology that connects us, the isolating conditions we face show no sign of letting up.

Epidemic Loneliness

Today, an epidemic of loneliness sequesters tens of millions of people. Barna's data shows that adults are *twice as likely* to say they are lonely compared to a decade ago; about one out of five Americans say they feel lonely. Regardless of the hundreds of millions of smartphones we've bought, apps we've loaded, posts we've written and read, and the "likes" and retweets we've given and received, we feel lonelier than ever.

Can you imagine how that's possible? You probably can. While our screens provide a plethora of opportunities to connect, we're spending more and more of our hours in digital bubbles, rarely interacting in a meaningful way with real human beings. Just read some of the stories of suicides or mass killings, and you'll find a common thread: tragic levels of isolation. Even before the era of ubiquitous digital connections, Robert Putnam's book *Bowling Alone* describes the collapse of America's social connectedness, in many ways predicting our emergence as an isolation nation.

Christians have an opportunity to provide a comprehensive solution to this kind of isolation by spending time together in and through the church.

Digital Strain

Another problem of isolation is that screens allow us to avoid the hard work of being human. Interpersonal interactions, mediated as they are by screens, often become rarer and more difficult. Breaking up via texts. Twitter fights. Facebook monologues. Cyberbullying. There is plenty of evidence that people will say and do things digitally that they would never consider saying or doing in person. Yet most people say they would rather use digital, text-based communication than talk things through in real life. We see this all the time in the business world, where workers would rather send an email than pick up the phone. "It's just easier. I don't want to bother them or be bothered."

Digital life strains families too. Given the addictive nature of screens, more tension exists in households when it comes to technology than ever before. Parents pounce on their kids ("No more screen time today!"). Children feel their parents are screen hypocrites ("Leave your work at the office! Put your phone down and listen to us!"). The subtitle of Jean Twenge's excellent book *iGen* says it all: *Why Today's Super-Connected Kids Are Growing Up Less Rebellious, More Tolerant, Less Happy—and Completely Unprepared for Adulthood—and*

What That Means for the Rest of Us. There are extreme challenges in raising relationally whole kids in the present digital environment. Churches need to provide structures that minimize digital strain in order to produce relationally whole, relationally enabled people.

Questioning the Meaning of Life

Another component of our isolating times is the popularization of nihilistic worldviews, which reject moral and religious underpinnings to life. Life is essentially meaningless. Take *13 Reasons Why*, which is a popular Netflix teen drama describing thirteen reasons why a young woman decides to commit suicide. The fictional young woman leaves a series of videos enumerating her reasons (most of which are based on real and heartbreaking relational breakdown) for making this "sensible" decision. It's a cold calculus that life can be weighed in the balance of the "reasons" to live or to take one's life. This was a wildly popular book and is now a wildly popular program, which algorithms recommend to multitudes of viewers each month.

At the other end of the spectrum, digital Babylon tempts us to believe that human bodies have no limitation. We can extend our lives and influence indefinitely. In the gaming world, we can bulk up or slim down, making our avatars anything we wish them to be. By way of social media and YouTube, we can extend our thoughts, our visages, and our brands around the world. The body seems to matter less and less as we embrace this practice of living in a variety of disembodied ways.

Christian relationships provide a deeper way to discover meaning in human life as well as the blessings and limitations of the human body, what the Catholic community calls the theology of the body.[5]

A My-Sized Life

Another contributing factor to this isolation nation has been the steady rise of individualization—everything is my-sized. As we described earlier, individuality can be a good thing, and God's love for individual persons is one of the most distinctive parts of Christian theology; each and every soul matters to God, and it should to us too.

Still, our my-sized world has led to an overwhelming me-first set of expectations, especially when so much of life is experienced through screens two feet from our faces. There's even a term for the reflective, self-focused output of the smartphone era: the selfie! Capture the perfect image of me, myself, and I. This is so strange that a time traveler from the past would wonder at our mental stability.

But almost all of us take selfies, don't we?

In what ways have the screen era and the selfie phenomenon contributed to the breakdown of community and a crisis of loneliness? One of the fascinating developments is the fact that Americans are highly likely to say their friendships are formed with people who are most like themselves—in terms of ethnicity, religion, education, faith. It's true that birds of a feather tend to flock together, but the digital commons allows us to hole up in our own nests.

The church can and must be a place that brings people together across differences and in pursuit of more than ourselves. But this isn't an easy or straightforward endeavor.

In fact, many people are extending their individualism to spirituality.

In a study we conducted for Navigators, *The State of Discipleship*, we discovered that people, especially young Christians, believe that discipleship can be accomplished as a solo effort.[6] For example, 41 percent of Christians say, "I believe my spiritual life is entirely private," and 37 percent say that they want to be discipled "on my own."

"Solo discipleship" may as well be an oxymoron, because those two words are completely antithetical, like pretty ugly, jumbo shrimp, a deafening silence, or acting naturally. Yet so often church is created for the individual. Songs are sung vertically to God; we no longer sing "horizontally" to one another. Even sacraments like baptism are often described in terms of individual spiritual journeys, disembodied from the corporate experience of the body of Christ. Both the vertical and the horizontal are important. A good litmus test is whether worship or baptism would be possible without other people in the pew. If you can do it on your own, it probably isn't church.

To disciple effectively in digital Babylon, we have to confront the myth of lone-wolf, do-it-yourself, sole-proprietorship discipleship. To do so, some churches have moved to a covenantal model of membership. To be a member of the Village Church in Texas, for example, a believer enters into a covenant similar to a marriage, with both sides making solemn promises before God, because "membership at the Village is participation in a family, a microcosm of the universal household of God. All members are united to Christ and thus to each other."[7]

In God (and Church) We Mistrust

A few years ago, the Barna team was conducting research among teenagers who had left the church. While interviewing a young woman about her relationships within the church before she left, David asked, "Did you have good friendships at the church?"

"No, not really. I guess a couple of my age group were my friends, but not close."

"None of the adults?"

"No."

"What about the youth pastor?"

"The youth pastor was paid to be my friend."

David needed a couple of seconds to catch his breath. "What do you mean?"

"That was part of his job. He's paid to be a marketer of church to teenagers."

Ouch.

That intense exchange and the one described at the beginning of this chapter exemplify the sediment of mistrust building up in and around the next generation. Beyond isolation, another layer to the relational pressures facing Gen Z and Millennials is skepticism about leaders and institutions that previously were seen as authoritative without question.

The stereotypes between generations can be barbaric. Ask a roomful of older adults what they think of Millennials, and you will see the mud start to sling. Interestingly, younger adults, while certainly not angels, are less likely to hold negative opinions and stereotypes of older adults than their parents and grandparents hold about them. For example, this percentage is nearly zero: Christians over the age of fifty who believe that Millennials are among the most generous or the most hospitable in their church. But Millennials are magnanimous when ascribing generosity or hospitality to Boomers.

In other words, when it comes to dredging up bad feelings, older adults are masterful. And yet our churches must be places that cut through generational clutter and reconcile people to one another in and through Christ. (We'll propose some ideas for how to do this in pages to come.)

Pastors are aging and thus have greater difficulty connecting with younger generations, if you believe the conventional wisdom that communicators ideally need to be within a ten-year age range of their audiences. It's not that older pastors are *unable* to connect with younger audiences; we just need leaders across *all* age ranges. We're finding, though, that younger leaders are increasingly rare. In a study conducted for Pepperdine University, Barna discovered that the typical Protestant pastor in the US today is fifty-four years old—ten years older than the average age of pastors in 1992.[8]

The industry of ministry leaders is aging. And that's a problem because without a sufficient supply of younger leaders advocating for the gospel—and for meaningful, intergenerational relationships in Christ—the church will struggle to raise enough leaders and future disciples.

Taking mistrust to an even deeper level are the brutal revelations of clergy abuse and the horror of #metoo and #churchtoo stories. Shining a light on these sickening injustices is good and healthy, albeit painful. Unfortunately, the negative perceptions produced by these situations often cast suspicion on tens of thousands of leaders who are not guilty, leading to further disengagement from the church community.

Church as Business

Our research has uncovered that many young Christians also mistrust the "big business" of church. These perceptions sound a note of caution not just to the biggest ministries and churches but to churches of any size. In our effort to achieve "success" as a church, are we sacrificing discipleship and the opportunity to transform people? In what ways can our churches be more human, more humanized? What is the relational IQ of our churches? We need to ask hard questions on this front because it matters. Could teens and young adults be getting the impression that staff are "paid to be their friend"? In what ways is the business of church contributing to relational mistrust?

By the way, we *should* run our churches in a transparent, efficient, and, yes, even businesslike way. But the driving ethos of the church should never feel corporate or stale. Our God is big enough to care about the hairs on each head and the condition of our souls; our experiences of church must embody this kind of personal and relational God.

Weaponized Humor

Another dimension of relational breakdown and mistrust in digital Babylon is the callousness of what we find entertaining or, more specifically, what we laugh at. God designed humor, and Scripture even describes it as a medicine. It plays a critical role in human life, sprinkling humility into arrogance and dousing anguish and anger with much-needed perspective. Satire, for instance, can provide corrective action to societal problems by speaking truth to power and helping to realign the imagination toward the good, true, and beautiful.

Yet Barna intends to conduct more research on the use and power of humor because we hypothesize that the kinds of things that are considered funny today are much more snarky and sarcastic than in the past. On the plus side, there has been a growing awareness that humor that denigrates race, sexuality, obesity, and disability is morally wrong. Still, consider that the kinds of programs we find entertaining often have a cynical way of portraying the world. The next generation has been raised on a steady diet of this kind of humor: *The Daily Show*, *The Office*, *Jackass*, and so on. Also consider the way Twitter or Facebook has led us to believe we are all effective comedians. Humor has been weaponized.

Think of Michael Scott from *The Office* television series. He is a self-important man who epitomizes the stupid things that bosses do and say. *The Office* is a "mockumentary" made to look like the real thing but told from a point of view that makes the *true enough* aspects of office life feel like a farce. One of the underlying messages of *The Office*—yes, there are messages in entertainment—is that workplace politics are so dysfunctional that surviving each day is the best one can hope for. We suspect that as members of today's generation ingest this kind of portrayal of working life, they can't help but change their engagement in real life for the worse, making them cynical and guarded, afraid to be openhanded and openhearted about contributing to a more functional workplace.

We are being conditioned to exhibit less confidence in others, particularly those in positions of authority. Digital Babylon frames our reality: people who are really, really, really earnest—like pastors—are probably nothing more than self-important people and perhaps even frauds. We are hearing from more pastors and youth pastors that their job as communicators is getting more difficult in part because people are more skeptical of the sage on the stage.

We contend that the changing role of humor contributes to a more anxious age in which we find reasons to *mis*trust one another and respond with sarcasm in the ordinary parts of life. As we disciple the next generation, how can we live with greater trust and openness toward one another?

Rediscovering Relationships in the Church

Mistrust and relational isolation cut at the heart of human and Christian community. To use a simple metaphor, the walls are higher and the barriers are thicker between us and meaningful relationships. And that means it's more difficult for us to find critical, livable answers to some of our hearts' deepest longings.

- Am I loved?
- Who are my friends?
- Does anyone care about me?

As we said earlier, the church can and should provide answers to the deepest questions of humanity in and through Jesus. In this case, our search for relational intimacy and supportive, others-oriented community is found in the church. As part of the community of Jesus, we bear one another's burdens. We experience love and intimacy. In short, we find that we are loved, we experience authentic friendship, and we discover people who care deeply about us.

In exile, the church can provide answers to a relationally hurting society. The Christian community today has an amazing opportunity to address the epidemic of isolation and counteract the atomizing effects of digital Babylon—and thereby diminish the mistrust and isolation we're all experiencing.

Did you catch that? The church can help fill a massive gap in our society: the desire to be loved, to be acknowledged for more than what we produce, to be known.

Resilient disciples have robust relationships in many different dimensions of their lives. In our survey, we inquired about relational connections without specifically talking about church, faith, or Christianity. As you can see in table 7, resilient disciples are far and away more relationally well-rounded than others their age.

More than three-quarters say they have "at least one close friend I trust with my secrets," "when growing up, I had close personal friends who were adults," and "I have someone in my life, other than family, who I can go to for advice on personal issues." Two-thirds of resilients strongly agree with the statements "My friends help me to be a better person" and "I have friends and family who are honest with me about my

Table 7. What Builds Resilient Disciples? Strong Relational Networks *Percentage who strongly agree with each statement*	Prodigals/ Ex-Christians	Nomads/ Unchurched	Habitual Churchgoers	Resilient Disciples
I have at least one close friend I trust with my secrets.	52%	53%	51%	83%
When growing up, I had close personal friends who were adults.	62%	60%	69%	81%
I have someone in my life, other than family, who I can go to for advice on personal issues.	49%	45%	47%	77%
My friends help me to be a better person.	34%	33%	42%	67%
I have friends and family who are honest with me about my weaknesses.	33%	34%	42%	66%
I am very content when I am by myself.	44%	37%	41%	58%
I wish I had more close friendships.	28%	35%	34%	43%

N = 1,514 US 18- to 29-year-olds who grew up as Christians
Source: Barna, February 2018

weaknesses." More than half firmly agree with the idea that "I am very content when I am by myself," which is another indicator of relational wholeness. Flashes of loneliness don't sneak up on them as often as others when they are alone. Finally, resilients are most likely to say, "I wish I had more close friendships"—an additional mark of an appropriate level of self-*insufficiency*.

In comparing resilient disciples to the other young adults who grew up as Christians, it's striking to see that being a resilient disciple, which is based on a set of questions about theology and faith engagement, correlates to overall relational well-being. Keep in mind, as we've cautioned before, that correlation doesn't imply causation; we don't know what factors come first. However, this kind of relational resilience is something all of us want, whether we're Christian or not. These young exemplars show us that a kind of relationally connected life is possible, even if they have room for growth too.

Christians can help to answer the deepest longings of our society for connection. Then instead of saying, "In God we mistrust," people might be able to honestly say, "In God and his people we trust." Helping people achieve connection is not easy, but there are intentional steps we can take to foster meaningful relationships.

As we turn to some of the practical ways to become this kind of relationally transforming community, we need to remind ourselves of one of the most common pitfalls: thinking this is no big deal. Relationships? Easy enough. Yep, we got that.

You probably don't. In our experience, it's especially easy for church leaders, pastors, and parents to assume that supportive relationships are already happening. Please do consider what's working and why, but also consider that your assumptions may not be as true as you'd like them to be. Relationships are easy to assume, especially when human beings show up for church events. Also, because pastors and church leaders tend to be more relationally minded, they can easily assume the same thing is happening for everyone else too.

With that in mind, let's dive into ways to build meaningful relationships.

Do the Work of Relational Health and Wholeness

The first step is to have a resilient, robust definition of meaningful relationships. Based on our research, here's what we'd suggest:

> Relationships are meaningful when
> we are devoted to fellow believers we
> want to be around and become.

Simple, right? But such relationships are more difficult than you'd think.

Saying we love other Christians is easy, but do we *like* being around them? That's the target. We want our young people to enjoy the time they spend with and around other church people. That will likely mean getting together outside of regularly scheduled worship and class times, doing the "stuff" of life together. Many churches focus on what happens during the weekend worship events, and insufficient time is spent working to facilitate experiences in which people grow to like being with one another.

Perhaps older adults could go to kids' soccer games and school plays (even if they aren't their own kids or grandkids).

We've heard of churches that help young people conduct video interviews with the older generations and then create a short film about the history of the church; that film is shown during a weekend worship service, reflecting the voices of the generations coming together.

In fact, making things together can be a powerful relationship builder. An older woman who volunteered in Mark's youth group was the quintessential TV homemaker with a dash of Betty White thrown in. She made individual birthday cakes for each of the students, specially decorated to reflect their personalities and interests.

A couple of the girls were gushing over how great the cakes tasted and asked her what mix she used. "Mix?!" she said, almost offended. "This doesn't come out of a box. I make it from scratch!"

The girls looked at each other and then asked, "What does 'from scratch' mean?"

What happened next were cooking lessons at that sweet lady's house. Every girl (and a few of the guys) learned how to bake cakes with ingredients they measured and sifted themselves. After a couple of classes, the kids wanted more, so she taught them how to make a complete Thanksgiving dinner— with gravy made from scratch.

Shared experiences of all types in which generations can connect—short-term mission and work-service trips, mentoring, back-to-school shopping, museum visits, and more— create opportunities for people to enjoy being together. This is something we should prioritize if we hope to help grow meaningful relationships for resilient disciples.

The second element of meaningful relationships is spending time with people we want to become. This looks like young

Christians hoping to emulate the lives, aspirations, and values of older generations. We recently came across a tweet that sums up what we should be after here: "The teenager who looks out over the congregation and thinks 'These are my people— I belong here' is most likely to look up and say, 'You are my God—I belong in your presence.'"[9]

How can we create such a compelling picture in our church communities?

One part of being healthy and whole is admitting when things aren't working. One year the youth pastor at Mark's church asked him to lead the senior class group, which in most youth programs sees a major drop-off in attendance over the course of the school year. Mark agreed. The first night he passed out index cards and asked the seventeen- and eighteen-year-olds to anonymously share something they wanted him to know but were reluctant to say out loud, thinking he would then be able to plan his programming for the year based on what was on their minds.

About half the cards had some variation of "I don't believe in God anymore; I'm just playing along until I graduate." So rather than planning a bunch of programs and activities, Mark spent the year listening to and talking with the seniors about their doubts. Nothing was off the table. And instead of shrinking, the senior class group grew. And grew. Today, over ten years later, most of those almost-thirty-year-olds are still walking with the Lord.

The resilient disciples we've talked to are surprisingly candid about their frustrations and disillusionment with their churches. Yet they haven't given in, for the most part, to cynicism. They've learned to talk about and process their feelings. Experienced a bad church leader? Join the club. Let's talk it through. Seen something in the church that burst your bubble? That's pretty normal. Let's get to the bottom of the illusions we hold about church and figure out what to do with the not-so-great feelings—together.

You may recall the story of Jim allowing a young woman to talk through an exceptionally bad mission trip with a bad leader. Unfortunately, those things happen. We can't hide them or bury the emotions. Jim told us, "I let her unload the emotional stuff with no challenges. Then after a long time of listening, I suggested that sometimes we need bad leaders in our lives so that we can clarify our own ideas and behaviors as leaders. I didn't try to defend the other leader, and I tried to move us past blame to more vulnerability."

We've all been disillusioned by someone. Getting past it, and even growing through it, involves talking it through, coming to a broader perspective, and agreeing on a way forward. The process of listening and redirecting the bitterness to more productive outcomes—through relationships—is an important way for resilience to grow.

Seek Specific Relational Outcomes

A second key to building meaningful relationships in exile is being intentional about the desired outcomes of our efforts. As we've argued, there are all sorts of land mines on the way to relational wellness. So we can't casually spend our weeks and months in digital Babylon—in the midst of crushing isolation and systemic mistrust—and hope to come out with meaningful relationships. We must be intentional about our goals.

We've seen some of those outcomes in our exploration of the relational wholeness exemplified by resilient disciples. Those specific outcomes are the kinds of things we should aspire to, especially as we consider how to boost the relational network of the next generation: a friend to confide in, adults who are considered friends, a wise adviser, someone who is honest about my weaknesses, a sense of being okay when I am alone.

In addition to general outcomes of friendship and supportive relationships, we discovered evidence that resilient disciples experience a very different kind of Christianity than do habitual churchgoers. Again, we can't say what comes first, but the gap is astounding. For example, 82 percent of resilients strongly agree that they are connected to a community of Christians, compared to only 33 percent of habitual churchgoers and just 7 percent of nomads (see table 6). That's a massive gap, and it suggests a very real difference in lived experiences. The top relational predictors of resilient Christians are these: I feel connected to a community of Christians; the church is a place where I feel I belong; I feel loved and valued in my church; I feel connected to people older than me in my church.

Faith communities and Christian households, then, must become resilient villages designed with outcomes in mind. Here are some of the things resilient disciples exemplify:

- I am confident in my relationships at church.
- I feel connected to people of all ages in my church.
- I am mentored by someone older, and I mentor someone younger.
- I know how to appropriately use digital tools to grow my relationships.
- I know to avoid digital tools when they inhibit my relationships.

By showing these outcomes, we hope you will begin to seek ways to achieve them with the young people you encounter in church, at a Christian school or college, or in your family. Evidence suggests that churches, schools, and families that produce resilient disciples have a clear set of well-articulated goals and outcomes in mind, and they run all their decisions through the grid of whether these outcomes will be gained by virtue of their time together.

A good starting place is asking the question "Where are we achieving these goals already?" If the answer is "Um, nowhere," then ask, "How can we modify existing programs or create new ones to achieve these goals?" The simple addition of meals before and after services could allow broader connections and opportunities to meet and connect with others.

Want to think even further outside the box? Imagine a church with no service and no stage. Yet you still have to accomplish your stated mission. What changes?

Pay Attention to Emotions

The places we want to go and the people we want to hang out with are full of feelings—and these can be positive, negative, or neutral. This is one of the things that most commonly defines the perceptions we uncovered in *unChristian* and *You Lost Me*: human beings are quick to discern when they don't feel welcome.

The implication is that we must assess and build an emotionally healthy context for relationships.[10] This happens (or doesn't) in our families. This occurs (or doesn't) in our churches. This is facilitated (or isn't) in our workplaces and institutional structures. We have a responsibility, whatever our age or role, to contribute to this kind of healthy environment.

Look at the data in table 8. Resilient disciples are much more likely than habitual churchgoers, nomads, or prodigals to describe emotionally positive experiences in the context of their churches. Interestingly, nomads are about the same as prodigals, which suggests that the emotional distance between nomads and the church is quite substantial.

Whatever the nature of a young person's spiritual journey, we can help to bridge the emotional gaps by using words that convey a warm emotional experience. "You are loved and valued here. You are family. We are brothers and sisters in Christ.

Table 8. **The Emotional Climate of Churches** Percentage who strongly agree with each statement	Prodigals/ Ex-Christians	Nomads/ Unchurched	Habitual Churchgoers	Resilient Disciples
Loved and valued.	23%	26%	50%	83%
Like I am part of a family.	18%	21%	47%	76%
Connected with those older than me.	20%	16%	31%	65%
Relief from the anxiety of daily life.	12%	18%	37%	63%
Connected with my peers.	15%	14%	36%	62%
Enabled to deal with life's challenges.	11%	16%	32%	59%
Understood for who I really am.	16%	11%	29%	54%
Supported by someone during a personal crisis.	12%	12%	28%	54%
Judged by others.	13%	1%	16%	9%
Disappointed by the hypocrisy of Christians.	18%	17%	12%	11%
Lonely and isolated.	11%	8%	8%	4%
Not spiritual enough.	10%	18%	14%	10%

N = 1,178 US 18- to 29-year-olds who grew up as Christians
Source: Barna, February 2018

Tell me how you're feeling. I am really sorry about how hard it is to grow up today, but you're safe here." As we mentioned, dealing frankly and openly with disappointment and dysfunction is helpful.

In addition to what we say, we can also build an emotionally healthy context by offering our most precious resources: our time and our attention. If you think about it, most of what church leaders are compensated for is running worship services and programs, which are important and valuable. And most of the ways we measure and experience "church" involve doing things *for* people, not necessarily being *with* people. We have to change this imbalance of program over presence. Doing so will help us create a healthier emotional climate, together.

When we talk to those who attend Christian colleges and universities, they say that one of the best parts of that experience is getting to know—and being known by—the professors and administration. Being invited to have a meal together. Getting to know them outside the classroom. Getting help sorting out difficulties they face. Students notice the people who care. And this is demonstrated by giving time and attention—the ministry of presence.

Even while experiencing better-than-average positive emotions, resilient disciples still show plenty of room for growth, and negative emotions aren't completely foreign to them. One out of ten feels they are not spiritual enough, and one out of nine says they are disappointed by the hypocrisy of Christians.

We need to evaluate and take action. What are the beneficial emotions people are feeling in my family/church, and how can I/we produce more of them? What are the negative, harmful emotions people are experiencing in my family/church, and how can I/we reduce them?

David used to have a professional coach, and whenever he brought up some negative emotions, she'd say, "David, that feels really sticky. Let's talk about that more." Another friend says, "David, don't take that situation personally. You need to find a better way of thinking about it." In each of these instances, the coach and the mentor helped identify the emotional context of what was happening—especially inside—in order to respond more effectively.

Now, we're not talking about simply trying to bring out happy thoughts, like passing out mood-altering drugs at church or plastering smiley emojis on our Sunday faces. Emotionally healthy contexts allow healthy expressions of all emotions. Be angry and do not sin, the Bible says (see Eph. 4:26). Joy and sadness go hand in hand (okay, that's from Pixar's *Inside Out*, but you get the picture). Emotions are a huge part of what it takes for us to feel less isolated, more trusting—and ultimately more Christian. Psychologist and theologian Richard Beck describes his experiences growing up in a particular denomination. Those formative experiences were powerful, he says: "Being 'Church of Christ' becomes etched into your limbic system. When you've worked through emotions of awkwardness as a child and adolescent you're not simply a member of the church of Christ intellectually, you're a member emotionally. That identity goes very, very deep."[11]

Be Vulnerable

One of the ways we break down walls of mistrust and isolation is to cultivate vulnerability, to interact with others without wearing masks or putting on pretenses. This kind of vulnerability has allowed Alcoholics Anonymous to thrive; meetings are a place where people can simply be, and are recognized for, who they are.

"Hi, my name is _____, and I'm an alcoholic."

It's deeply ironic that in a society more connected than ever, in a culture in which we can pick up a phone and contact any number of friends or "friends," we are feeling less relationally fulfilled. In the *Atlantic*, Stephen Marche wrote:

> We are living in an isolation that would have been unimaginable to our ancestors, and yet we have never been more accessible. Over the past three decades, technology has delivered to us a world in which we need not be out of contact for a fraction of a moment. In 2010, at a cost of $300 million, 800 miles of fiber-optic cable was laid between the Chicago Mercantile Exchange and the New York Stock Exchange to shave three milliseconds off trading times. Yet within this world of instant and absolute communication, unbounded by limits of time or space, we suffer from unprecedented alienation. We have never been more detached from one another, or lonelier.[12]

According to one major study, about 20 percent of Americans (or sixty million people) are unhappy with their lives because of loneliness.[13]

The church has a unique opportunity to break through this loneliness and introduce real vulnerability by returning to our roots as a confessional community. When we talk about our sin that so easily entangles, we create connections with others that transcend the transaction of posting a selfie in exchange for a few likes.

A big part of vulnerability in a Christian community is the ability to talk about and wrestle with doubt. *You Lost Me* found that a significant percentage of young people leave the church because they feel it is doubt-less and incapable of helping them handle their doubt. They feel that instead of engaging them in their space of questioning, the church tries to steamroll and look past their legitimate doubts.

In contrast, environments that help young people effectively talk through their doubt are places young people love to be. For example, Christian schools that provide forums for students to discuss their doubt and ask questions and that convey the idea that doubt is not the opposite of faith become places where young people feel accepted and involved.

Creating meaningful relationships within the church can't be simply about encouragement or positivity. Meaningful relationships often arise out of difficult disagreements along our journey together. Part of being vulnerable is sticking around long enough to work them out.

Take Digital Sabbaths

When a friend recently took his family to a mountain cabin for their annual getaway, they left all their screens at home. As they pulled into the cabin's driveway after a two-hour drive, he asked his children how it felt to be in the car for that long without playing on any of their devices.

"Freedom!" shouted one of his smiling kids.

"It kind of feels like we're a family again," another said.

Could it be that our screens are having a similar effect on our churches—causing us to feel less like family?

Andy Crouch argues in *The Tech-Wise Family* that our screens should wake up after we do and go to bed before we do.[14] What if we deliberately put our screens away one hour a day, one day a week, and one week a year? What if our churches and youth groups taught young people how to have conversations in real life?

Great things are available to Christians on their smartphones: innumerable translations of the Bible, study guides, alarms that can serve as reminders to pray, and instant access to videos of helpful talks given by spiritual leaders. But addiction to screens is also possible. In one Denmark study, over one thousand participants quit Facebook for one week—and reported significant increases in their level of life satisfaction. They also discovered that frequent Facebook users were more likely than those who use it less often to feel angry (20 percent versus 12 percent), depressed (33 percent versus 22 percent), and worried (54 percent versus 41 percent).[15]

We need to practice consistent Sabbaths away from our screens if we are going to inhabit a better mental space and connect more fruitfully with those around us.

Help Young People Identify Faith Champions

Each young disciple needs champions outside their immediate family who follow Jesus and can sponsor their spiritual development—other adults who can shape them, speak into their lives, and help them develop their gifts. Based on Barna's research, David is working to deepen this area for his own kids.

One daughter, Annika, has a wonderful friend named Ava, a young mom. The two of them go running together, and my daughter spends time with their family. They text back and forth a lot and have deep, important conversations.

My other daughter, Emily, is under the wing of our friends Andy and Catharine. She's gone on several trips with them, and they enjoy cool things centered on food, travel, art, and literature. It's been remarkable to see how strong their connection has become.

My son, Zack, has made numerous connections with adults, all of whom have helped him navigate his life. We recently went through a family crisis, and they helped him deal with some of the grief we were all experiencing.

We can't overstate the importance of these relationships with adults outside the family, especially as children move through their teen years. There are some things kids simply won't be able to hear from or work through with their parents. High-quality, Jesus-seeking adults in their lives can help keep them involved in church, be people they want to be around, and provide them with examples they can emulate.

Realize the Crucial Role of Mentors

Intergenerational relationships are central to the concepts we've been describing, and these kinds of relationships don't usually happen by accident. They require intentional planning and consistent effort from everyone involved.

Table 9 reveals that resilient disciples are more intergenerationally connected than their peers. However, there is room for growth even among resilient exemplars.

Four out of ten resilient disciples (more than double of any of the other groups) have had an adult mentor at church, someone other than a staff member. More than half of resilient disciples look to an older person for advice when making difficult decisions.

Of course, there are inherent challenges to these relationships, and one such challenge is that older adults must have some interest in becoming like the next generation. They must see strengths in young exiles that their own generation does not have and recognize that the new generation offers a different way forward. We call this "reciprocal mentoring." The church needs young exiles, not so we can re-indoctrinate them but so that they can teach us, show us, what it means to grow in digital Babylon.

Exiles have to work out friendships and relationships in an entirely different context, something emphasized in 1 Peter, a letter addressed "to God's elect, exiles scattered throughout the provinces of Pontus, Galatia, Cappadocia, Asia and Bithynia" (1:1 NIV). It offers encouragement for the challenges that come with living away from home. The writer implores God's people to remain faithful, to live holy lives, and to prepare

Table 9. What Builds Resilient Disciples? Intergenerational Community *Percentage who strongly agree with each statement*	Prodigals/ Ex-Christians ✘	Nomads/ Unchurched ◉	Habitual Churchgoers	Resilient Disciples
I feel valued by the people in my life who are older than me.	24%	26%	37%	65%
I welcome positive criticism from those who are older than me.	29%	30%	35%	60%
I often look to those who are older than me for advice when I need to make difficult decisions.	21%	25%	37%	56%
I mainly trust people my own age for insights and advice.	12%	9%	20%	24%
Older people don't seem to understand the pressures my generation is under.	33%	24%	25%	24%

N = 1,514 US 18- to 29-year-olds who grew up as Christians
Source: Barna, February 2018

themselves for suffering. But he also has very specific relational exhortations:

> Above all, love each other deeply, because love covers over a multitude of sins. Offer hospitality to one another without grumbling. Each of you should use whatever gift you have received to serve others, as faithful stewards of God's grace in its various forms. If anyone speaks, they should do so as one who speaks the very words of God. If anyone serves, they should do so with the strength God provides, so that in all things God may be praised through Jesus Christ. To him be the glory and the power for ever and ever. Amen. (4:8–11 NIV)

Christian exiles, no matter the era, must be reminded to offer hospitality instead of grumbling, to speak responsibly, to serve one another well, and to operate within their gifts. This is how a new life of meaningful relationships can be forged together, even in exile.

■ ■ ■

David Medders has a folksy, completely authentic charm. He is uber-friendly. His Alabama accent disarms and draws people in. He adores his family and his grandchildren, serving them and praying for them and anguishing over their highs and lows. And David loves Jesus; it oozes out of everything he says and does. One time he skipped an entire afternoon conference session just to answer a young girl's questions about faith. He had never met Annika Kinnaman before, but he focused in on her as if she were his own granddaughter.

I (David) met David Medders almost a decade ago in Orlando, Florida. He and his colleague Ralph had asked me to conduct a seminar for Christian college students. I poured my heart into it. My talks lasted most of the morning and afternoon. The students seemed engaged and interested as I described sampling error with stats-packed PowerPoint slides.

At the end of my nearly endless stream of data insights, when you could almost see visible z's rising from the audience members' heads, David stood up in front of the seventy-five young leaders sitting in the room. He broke the stats-induced haze with a few jokes, to great effect. The room filled with laughter.

Then David switched gears. "I'd like to personally repent for my generation, the Boomers, and how we've let these negative perceptions take root. Did you see all those negative perceptions your generation has of the church? Hypocritical. Judgmental. Antihomosexual."

He paused as he struggled to catch his voice. "This happened on our watch . . . on my generation's watch . . . and I am so sorry."

I've rarely seen a room full of *anyone*, much less college students who've endured a stats-laden speech from a droning research geek, get so quiet and focused. They couldn't believe what they were hearing. *I* couldn't. David was apologizing for his entire generation. He continued for nearly ten minutes, sharing heartfelt concern for their dilemma, their future, and their faith, and the emotions of many students began to well up as tears.

Next, he prayed. And he asked students to pray. That hotel in Orlando became someplace holy that afternoon.

The reality of vulnerability.

The power of confessional community.

The presence of Jesus working in hearts.

One thing is as sure as my friend's southern drawl: David Medders is a Christ follower I want to be around, and the kind I hope to become.

To Ground and Motivate an Ambitious Generation, Train for Vocational Discipleship

Vocational discipleship means knowing and living God's calling, especially in the arena of work, and right-sizing our ambitions to God's purposes.

Charles Roven, producer of *Wonder Woman*, *The Dark Knight*, and *American Hustle* (to name a few), once attended a wedding at which Mark was the officiant. Dax Matlock, Mark's son, had recently completed a summer internship at Chuck's production company in Hollywood, and Mark wanted to thank Chuck for contributing to his son's development. It had been a good prevocational experience, something Dax would never forget.

As Chuck and Mark chatted, they began to talk about the next generation. Mark was fascinated by Chuck's perspective, especially in light of all the generational and vocational research taking place at Barna. Chuck considers himself an adherent to the values of old-school Hollywood, even though he's producing some of the films most appreciated by the next generation. He goes way back. (Chuck got his start as a stunt surfer on the original *Hawaii 5-0* during a gap year before starting college.) He believes people should pay their dues when they come into the industry and typically promotes only from within his company—a pretty amazing thing to know when one is starting as an intern. Dax's experience is a perfect example. As an intern, he began by making coffee and making copies. But eventually, he also got to read scripts and see how they are evaluated for production.

In many ways, Chuck's view on paying dues is boilerplate Boomer philosophy that many apply to every arena of life, whether they are talking business or leadership, income or happiness, marriage or church. If you are new, you work harder than anyone else doing the things no one else wants to do, and you work your way up from there. If you are young, you can't possibly deserve anything other than an entry-level position, and the only thing that moves you up the ladder is time served. Chuck and his generation see this way of doing things as an opportunity for people to acquire knowledge from experience, knowledge they can't acquire any other way—some might call it wisdom.

Mark recently shared Chuck's sentiment about paying dues and working your way up from the bottom with a roomful of Boomer executives, and they all nodded wildly, like bobbleheads on the dashboard of a car on an unpaved back road. They also agreed with the following statements:

- The next generation doesn't want to pay their dues.
- Millennials want more responsibility than they deserve.
- They want opportunity before they're ready for it.

Not long after, relaxing over Labor Day weekend with Dax and his film student buddies—each of them balancing on the edge between Millennial and Gen Z—Mark asked them to talk about the view of these executives from *their* vantage point. Most had just finished internships and had experienced for themselves the "old-school" way of thinking. How did they feel about putting in their time, waiting in the queue, and paying their dues?

"The old school is dead," said one, shrugging with indifference. "Maybe not today or even in five years, but eventually . . ." He trailed off and then said, "The rules are different now."

Cue the clash of generations in the workplace.

▪▪▪

Here we glimpse the fourth domain of resilient discipleship: the world of work—how we think about and plan for what we do with our lives, discover our callings, find meaning, climb the ladder, achieve our ambitions, and become successful. Our work lives become the crucible in which much of our faith is tested and refined. In the arena of work and calling, we live our identity, deploy discernment, generate relationships, and pursue significance in the world. *Thus, the fourth way to build resilience in digital Babylon is through vocational discipleship.*

You've probably been nodding along during previous chapters of this book. Experience Jesus? Check. Cultural discernment? Right. Meaningful relationships? Makes sense. But vocational discipleship? What the blazes is that? Let's define it this way:

> Vocational discipleship means knowing and living God's calling—understanding what we are made to do—especially in the arena of work, and right-sizing our ambitions to God's purposes.

This may not be a concept you've encountered before. That's because Barna researchers invented the phrase based on the last decade of studying what works in discipleship. Even if it's a new concept, though, we're guessing you're already doing some of what we mean by it. And whether or not you've heard of it, it's vitally important.

The church desperately needs a richer theology of faith and faithfulness in life's complex callings, and we need to unite generations' seemingly disparate ways of understanding vocation. Vocational discipleship is crucial as we seek to raise Millennials and Gen Z disciples—but it is essential to build robust faith in older generations as well. How can we facilitate vocational discipleship within our church communities when the generations that need one another are coming from such wildly different places?

Let's explore what the research shows about eighteen- to twenty-nine-year-olds who embody resilient discipleship (see tables 10 and 11).

- *Resilient disciples are God-centered in their thinking about work and calling.* For example, 94 percent strongly agree that they want to use their "unique talents and gifts to honor God." That's one of the highest reported levels of agreement resilient disciples show for *anything*—and they're enthusiastic about many things related to their faith! Nearly nine out of ten say, "God designs each person with a unique calling for their life." Eight out of ten firmly agree that "all the work I do is important to God." These God-centered perspectives differentiate resilient disciples from their Christian peers.

- **Resilient disciples believe integrity in the workplace matters.** This is no small thing. In a culture that values

Table 10. **What Builds Resilient Disciples? A Well-Developed Theology of Work and Calling** *Percentage who strongly agree with each statement*	Prodigals/ Ex-Christians	Nomads/ Unchurched	Habitual Churchgoers	Resilient Disciples
I want to use my unique talents and gifts to honor God.	13%	31%	51%	94%
Christians are called to do their work with integrity, no matter the type of work.	17%	37%	53%	89%
God designs each person with a unique calling for their life.	23%	42%	56%	87%
I believe that all the work I do is important to God.	17%	32%	46%	82%
My church does a good job of helping me understand how to live out my faith in the workplace.	7%	11%	41%	72%
I do not have to work in a ministry to be working for God's kingdom.	33%	46%	51%	69%

N = 1,514 US 18- to 29-year-olds who grew up as Christians
Source: Barna, February 2018

getting ahead at any cost, resilient disciples are distinct from the norm: 89 percent say that "Christians are called to do their work with integrity, no matter the type of work." Just half of habitual churchgoers, one-third of nomads, and one-sixth of prodigals agree. Resilients are also much more likely to say that they conduct themselves in the workplace knowing that others are watching. If you're an employer, which kind of young adult would you prefer to hire?

• *Resilient disciples say that their churches help them live out their faith in the workplace.* Nearly three-quarters of exemplars say that their churches do a good job assisting them in this way, compared to two out of five habituals

Table 11. **Resilient Disciples Are More Engaged in Their Workplaces** _Percentage who strongly agree with each statement_	Prodigals/ Ex-Christians	Nomads/ Unchurched	Habitual Churchgoers	Resilient Disciples
I conduct myself in the workplace knowing that others are watching me.	37%	40%	48%	80%
God has called me to my current work.	12%	15%	31%	64%
The work I do at my job aligns with the person God has made me to be.	13%	17%	36%	63%
I am excited about my career path.	41%	34%	44%	61%
The work I do at my job is making a positive impact in the world.	34%	24%	39%	60%
I find fulfillment in my current workplace because I am able to use my God-given talents.	15%	18%	36%	57%

N = 1,019 US 18- to 29-year-olds who grew up as Christians
Source: Barna, February 2018

and only a small portion of nomads. One of the questions our research cannot answer is whether resilients get more out of their church experience because of an innate posture toward faith or because effective churches help resilients cultivate such a posture. Probably it is some of both.

- *The sacred-secular divide does not factor much into the thinking of resilient disciples.* Many Christians seem to be under the impression that some jobs are more important to God than others. Ministers and missionaries, for example, are doing more important work than accountants and researchers. Most theologians disagree this is the case, biblically speaking; instead, all work is dignified in God's eyes if it's done with the right motives and with good, true, and beautiful outcomes in mind. A majority of resilients, in contrast to many others, say that "I do not have to work in ministry to be working for God's kingdom."

- *Resilient disciples are more satisfied in their careers.* In addition to maintaining a richer theology of work, resilients also tend to report greater career satisfaction. For instance, they are more likely than their peers to report excitement about their career path (61 percent); to believe their job is making a positive impact in the world (60 percent); and to find fulfillment in their workplace because they are using their God-given talents (57 percent). Resilient disciples have room to grow in these areas, but they are already doing strikingly better than habitual churchgoers. They seem more ready to integrate their faith and their work, and that's what vocational discipleship is all about.

Why Vocational Discipleship?

A friend of ours has a son, Keaton, who created a PowerPoint life plan at the age of eight that we think is the most awesome thing in the world.[1] David told Keaton's dad he has a standing job offer. Keaton, that is. Not his dad.

Keaton has ten life goals. Here they are, in his words:

1. I want to grow up to be a nice Christian man.
2. I want to get a nice wife.
3. I want to get a good job, one that I like.
4. I want to have two kids, each boys, two years apart.
5. I want to grow as close as I can get to God.
6. I want to make more and more friends as I grow.
7. I want to work hard in school.
8. Believe in God wherever I go.
9. Teach my kids about God and help them live their lives as best as they can.
10. Do not give up on life.

He was eight!

On the next slide, Keaton listed possible careers: engineer, architect, hockey player, or Lego designer at Legoland in California or Florida.

Maybe you're wondering where we're going with this. What does an eight-year-old's vocational wish list have to do with discipleship?

Because we're trying to be more like Jesus, we'll answer your question with a few questions of our own.

If this family showed up at your church, would Keaton, aspiring to be an engineer, an architect, or a Lego designer, find a place he could be mentored and developed into the kind of person he is meant to be? Or would that kind of mentoring happen only by accident? How old does Keaton have to be before your church community "cares" about what he is made to do? About his work? About his perspectives on service and generosity? About integrity in the workplace?

We are convinced, based on mountains of data, that most churches ignore these topics among the young. It's a huge blind spot. Too often church leaders pay attention to vocation only when it relates to how already-successful people can serve the church. We need to back up the train all the way to the station. Every person in the church, even and especially those under eighteen, is designed by God to do his work in the world. Shouldn't their Christian community help them discern and live out that calling? Of course!

This is one of the key opportunities presented to the twenty-first-century church: to infuse the vocational imaginations of this new generation with the purposes of God; to help them understand that God has made them *for* something; to learn from and emulate the integrated faith-work profile that resilient disciples display.

An Ambitious Generation

Fame has become something of a North Star for many young people. One of the random facts the Barna team discovered is that 26 percent of teenagers think they will definitely or probably be famous by the time they turn twenty-five.[2] This is a side effect of life in digital Babylon, and the allure of "making it" on YouTube is strong. (We can laugh at the improbabilities of fame and fortune, but the truth is that some in this generation *will* become rich and/or famous. There are twentysomethings in Mark's church who are already million-aires. As Dax and his friends intuit, the world is changing and the rules are being rewritten. We will come back to this idea of fame and success in a bit when we talk about the right-sizing of ambition.)

Success is of central importance to this generation. Most teens tell us their top goals are to complete their education and to land a "great-paying job" where they "can make a dif-ference." Make no mistake, vocation is more important to Millennials and Gen Z than popular generational myths might lead us to believe. The world of work, business, (self-) employment, and earning is taking primacy of place, in part because young adults are pushing back the demographic markers of adulthood. Twentysomethings are marrying and having children later, giving them more of their twenties and thirties to focus on work and making the workplace their primary social hub.

The world of work is changing for the next generation. It's actually changing for all of us, but the youngest feel these shifts most potently. They're more engaged in the gig economy, mak-ing a little money here and a little money there, often as self-employed entrepreneurs—testing many waters and spending more time evaluating what aspects of their calling are impor-tant to them. They tend to engage less in the traditional work-force, so they're more concerned about creating a personal brand to take with them wherever they go. They are children of the Great Recession, so they're sensitive to what a downturn in the economy might mean for their careers.

They want to succeed in a job or a business that brings meaning to their lives. They would rather be their own boss.

They want to avoid positions that lead to the kinds of financial disasters their parents experienced.

This generation is ambitious, and it also turns out that the goals their Christian parents have for them are mostly indistinguishable from the goals non-Christian parents have for their children.[3] Teens' and young adults' ambitions for career, success, good grades, performance, and so on come *from* somewhere. With regard to educational and vocational hopes and dreams for their children, there is very little to differentiate Christians from non-Christians.

Those of us who are spiritual guides for the next generation must take a good, long look in the mirror to see how we are making faith more difficult for growing disciples. Are our goals for the next generation more about how our kids make us feel than about what God is calling them to do and be? In order to raise resilient *young* disciples, we must become resilient *older* disciples. If our aspirations for our children and grandchildren do not reflect godly ambition, living out God's purposes in their lives is harder for them than it has to be.

All these factors combine with the consumerism and get-aheadism of digital Babylon to create a generation of ambitious, success-oriented go-getters. If we don't invest in them as vocational disciples, we're going to lose their hearts. We're going to lose their minds. We're going to lose their irreplaceable contribution to the Christian community.

But if we can engage them vocationally and equip them for a life of kingdom-centered work, we will see them bless and change the culture of their workplaces and, ultimately, the world. What an incredible responsibility. What an amazing opportunity.

What Vocational Discipleship Is Not

Before we go too much further, let's lock something down. Vocational discipleship is not preaching success. It's not offering career advice to help young people land lucrative jobs, get wealthy and comfortable, buy nice things, and retire early with all the toys in the world. They are already ambitious; they don't need us throwing (unbiblical) gas on the fire. Something they *do* need is preparation for the seasons when they aren't as successful as they expect to be. When they don't get that promotion. When they have a conflict at work. When they fail—which they definitely will, at one time or another—and have to begin again.

As we've mentioned, the Kinnamans are really into Ecclesiastes. They are a driven family. Whether talking about grades or sports or any other activity, the Kinnamans are in it to win it. Reading a chapter of Ecclesiastes at dinner, being reminded that much of what we do on earth is fleeting, pushes reset. It's like putting on glasses that bring into focus how dysfunctional ambition can become.

This is one part of right-sizing ambition, a phrase included in our definition of vocational discipleship. The next generation of Christians (and the rest of us) needs grounding in what Jesus says about success: seek first the kingdom of God and all the rest will be added to you (Matt. 6:33).

What's My Calling?

At Barna, we've been thinking about and asking questions concerning vocation for almost fifteen years. Even early on, we thought discipling people around their calling presented the church with an opportunity, and we've only become more convinced as the years have passed.

More recently, as we zeroed in on this idea of what it takes to form resilient disciples, we asked Millennials, "What do you want to do in life?" We categorized their answers into different buckets, and what we found surprised us.

In the first big bucket, we placed our entrepreneurs. Nearly one half of all respondents are interested in careers related to entrepreneurship. They want to be marketers, business leaders, finance experts, and business owners. They want to start their own nonprofit organizations, be their own boss, and operate outside of traditional employment structures.

In the second bucket are the science minded, those interested in science, technology, engineering, and math (STEM). Nearly half of all young people express interest in this realm of work.

Finally, a third of respondents are interested in creative careers such as design, filmmaking, journalism, literature, fine arts, and performance arts. (Responders could pick more than one vocational aspiration, which is why the totals add up to more than 100 percent.)

Skye Jethani, a friend who has written quite a bit about vocation, says that he believes God designed work for three primary reasons. "This is exciting," Skye said when he saw how we'd broken down young people's aspirations, "because those buckets correspond to the three things work is designed for: to create beauty, to cultivate abundance, and to generate order."

This is one way to envision how God has wired human calling: to create beauty (creative careers), to cultivate abundance (entrepreneurial careers), or to generate order (STEM careers). Shouldn't we as the church be first in line to mentor young people as they walk into these kinds of God-ordained callings?

Connecting Desired Careers with God's Design for Work

Vocational discipleship involves being aware of the career aspirations of teens and young adults in our communities, and helping them to connect those goals with how God designed work. Nearly half of teens and young adults are interested entrepreneurial careers. About half aspire to science-minded careers. And one-third say they'd like to pursue a creative career such as journalism, art, music, graphic design, culinary arts, fashion, interior design, and so on.*

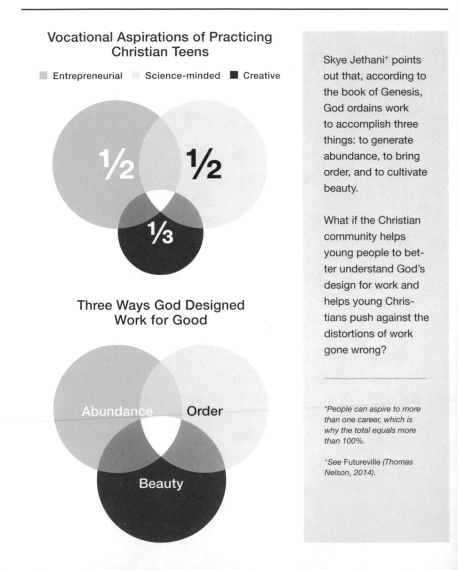

Vocational Aspirations of Practicing Christian Teens

■ Entrepreneurial   ■ Science-minded   ■ Creative

½   ½   ⅓

Three Ways God Designed Work for Good

Abundance   Order   Beauty

Skye Jethani[+] points out that, according to the book of Genesis, God ordains work to accomplish three things: to generate abundance, to bring order, and to cultivate beauty.

What if the Christian community helps young people to better understand God's design for work and helps young Christians push against the distortions of work gone wrong?

*People can aspire to more than one career, which is why the total equals more than 100%.

[+]See Futureville (Thomas Nelson, 2014).

There's a distinctly Christian way to think about vocation and work, and it isn't only for the next generation! It's for all of us. Christian vocation is about discovering what God is calling us to do and learning how to contribute to the work he is already doing and wants to do—including his work *in our workplaces*. Christians should be the ones in every workplace who resolve conflict, help their coworkers deal with grief and loss, and shine a gentle light of truth on our brokenness as coworkers, bosses, and employees.

Young Christians are hungry to think spiritually about the issues of our day. They long to find out what it means to follow Jesus in the workplace. This reawakening of the vocational imagination is deeply spiritual work. Awakening it in young disciples will propel more and more of them toward resilience.

The Power of Vocation and Calling

Most children, by the time they reach the age of nine or ten (and often earlier), exhibit quite an imagination when it comes to possible occupations. (For example, David was fairly certain that by his mid-40s he would already have retired from a successful career in the NBA—plans that would have come to fruition if athletic ability weren't a prerequisite.) Ask any child what they want to be when they grow up, and you'll get practical answers (doctor, lawyer, teacher), statistical anomalies (astronaut, professional athlete), and the downright fanciful (unicorn tamer, time traveler, superhero, owner of a butterfly store). There's something in each of us, even early on, that causes us to dream about what we'll do with our lives.

What's the church connection? We have an opportunity to connect with the next generations *when they are young* to help shape their godly imagination for what they might accomplish. Again, what an incredible opportunity!

Imagine if we could awaken in all God's children what resilient disciples say about their own lives.

- I see how my faith and my work are inseparable.
- I know how to help others discover who God made them to be.
- I am not just a consumer but a maker, a creator.
- I feel confident about the future because I know God will provide.

A worthy goal for our churches is for every young person to grow up able to say, "I know who God has created me to be and how my purpose fits with his plans for the world." What can we do to influence each and every young person in our faith communities to be able to say that with complete confidence?

It's rare to find a church that fully integrates vocational discipleship into its vision of making disciples. (So if this concept is new to you, you're not alone.) However, we *are* seeing more churches move into this arena, offering clear and tangible guidance on calling, career, and vocation. More youth and college leaders than ever are talking about issues of science, entrepreneurship, and creative careers. Youth and young adult church leaders are inviting professionals in to talk about their work and to form mentoring groups. The idea that purpose should be connected to a person's faith journey isn't quite as rare as it was even a decade ago. Still, there is much work to do.

For their part, a majority of resilient disciples report four outcomes of their engagement with church: (1) they better understand their purpose in life; (2) they view their gifts and passions as part of God's calling; (3) they have learned how the Bible applies to their field or interest area; and (4) they are better able to live out their faith in the workplace (see table 12). (Again, we can't be sure from this research alone if resilient disciples receive these benefits from their churches because they are somehow unique or

Table 12. How Churches Develop the Next Generation Vocationally

Which of the following, if any, have you personally experienced in your church, parish, or faith community? Please mark any that apply. And if none apply, please feel free to mark that.	Prodigals/ Ex-Christians	Nomads/ Unchurched	Habitual Churchgoers	Resilient Disciples
I better understand my purpose in life.	24%	27%	46%	74%
I have learned to view my gifts and passions as part of God's calling.	19%	21%	35%	67%
I have learned how the Bible applies to my field or interest area.	10%	14%	26%	57%
I am better able to live out my faith in the workplace.	13%	12%	29%	56%
I received guidance on what schools or colleges to attend.	9%	9%	19%	28%
I have access to leadership training for my job through my church.	8%	6%	15%	25%
I have received a scholarship for college through my church.	4%	4%	13%	11%

N = 1,178 US 18- to 29-year-olds who grew up as Christians
Source: Barna, February 2018

because their churches have been intentional in this area; it's probably a bit of both.)

Less common outcomes among resilient disciples include receiving a scholarship for college through their church, leadership training for their job through their church, or guidance concerning what school or college to attend. Interestingly, these outcomes are some of the few instances in which resilient disciples are not much different from habitual churchgoers. In other words, the practical sides of education and job training are missing in action from many churches' thinking about vocational discipleship.

Here are some ways churches can develop the next generation vocationally.

Host a Vocation Bible School

Churches around the world put on Vacation Bible School. They set aside a week in the summer (or maybe spring break), invite all the neighbor kids, and engage them with Bible stories and life lessons they will remember for a long time to come.

What if we put on a *Vocation* Bible School?

We could plan talks and activities for children, youth, and young adults that challenge how they think about making a living, that introduce biblical ideas about vocation, and that set them on a path toward meaningful work. Could we help them experience both the spiritual vitality that comes from following Jesus *and* the vibrancy of discovering what he created them to do?

Young people today are children of *Shark Tank*. They are full of new ideas and fabulous concepts that are so far outside our box we can't even see them. Of course, not every Millennial or Gen Z teen is interested in entrepreneurship—but a huge portion of them are, so let's help them work that muscle. Let's invite them to create organizations and businesses and products that extend and strengthen God's kingdom.

A Vocation Bible School could be something that appeals to people at various stages, from elementary school to junior high, high school, and college. And many adults could use a Vocation Bible School to talk about why it is they do what they do.

Vocation must become something we talk about more. And we're not talking about small-talk questions like "What do you do?" but intentionally dialoguing about faithfulness in all of life's complex callings.

That's a good definition of vocation. It's not just the work we do. It's not just a career, a job, or a profession. Vocation is being faithful in life's complex callings.

Invest Real Resources into Building Young Leaders

The pipeline of young leaders who are ready, willing, and able to direct churches, Christian nonprofits, and ministry organizations is shrinking. Ten to twenty years down the line, who will lead the institutions that shape and serve the Christian community, including media, publishing, education, relief and development, and more?

We must develop a more robust pipeline of young leaders. Terry Stokesbary and Steve Moore have been doing this in the Pacific Northwest for many years and are great models for the rest of us. They developed a program called Vision & Call that trains hundreds of Christian college students in a two-year internship program. These students work in various Christian organizations and come together for training and development. Some of the richest times David has had as a teacher have been with these young leaders, answering their eager, honest, hopeful questions.

One commitment we can make to vocationally disciple the next generation is to provide financial means for them to study and experience the world, helping young leaders find their place beyond high school youth group. David's wife, Jill, received a multiyear scholarship from her church to attend a college affiliated with her church's denomination. Her scholarship increased every year, so she had an incentive to stay in the same school and finish her degree. Much of who she is today, as a Christian and as a leader, came from the investment her church made in her as a future leader.

We must renew our commitment and make similar investments in the future.

Don't Count Out Christian Education

One of the most important features of the vocational landscape is educational institutions. These include schools, colleges, universities, training programs, online courses, and so on, as well as the people who inhabit them—teachers and students, the learned and the learning, educators and apprentices. In the best institutions, the line between the latter and the former (those instructing and those receiving instruction) is not impermeable.

We have become big advocates of the special role Christian education can play in shaping young hearts and minds. Public schools can be a rich proving ground for faithful Christians, and there are millions of public school educators whose faithful presence is a shining example of following Jesus. David's good friends LaDonna and Eddie Ramos are such people; they pour out blood, sweat, and tears for students in Oxnard, California. So don't get us wrong: public schools are not the enemy.

However, remember the tables you've seen in this book that show how many hours youth take in spiritual content and how many hours of other content they consume per year? Public schools offer no way to increase the number of hours students are trained to think *Christianly*. Christian schools offer much greater exposure to deeper, sturdier Christian formation. Learning cultural discernment and teaching vocational discipleship—along with the other practices—come a bit more naturally in a Christian educational environment.

Get a Mentor, Be a Mentor

Mark was being headhunted by a couple of ministry organizations. That was flattering and all, but he found himself asking, "Why are you looking at somebody like me who's almost fifty when you really need someone in their thirties?"

The reason? Experience. Gravitas. Wisdom. Wisdom that somebody in their mid- to late forties has more of just because they have logged more hours on the time card, regardless of inherent talent or formal education. One of our definitions of wisdom is "pattern recognition." Someone who's been working for fifteen, twenty, thirty-five years simply has a deeper well of patterns to reference and recognize.

Many young exiles have incredible ideas and drive, but they lack pattern recognition. How can older generations help those who want to move higher more quickly than they're actually able? Is making them put in their time or pay their dues the only or best way?

There is a human, church-driven approach to helping people discover their God-given purpose and wisely answering their vocational questions: mentoring. In mentoring, wisdom—pattern recognition—is passed on and provoked

163

through meaningful intergenerational relationships. (Hey, we've seen those before!)

We feel so strongly about the discipleship potential of mentoring that we included a special section on the topic at the end of this chapter. Here, in this section, we dig into the mentoring mind-set, the *whys* of mentoring; there you'll find the *whats*.

Resilient disciples, as we've seen, are much more likely than their peers to see and to seek wisdom—including positive criticism and input on difficult decisions—from older adults. Of course, as in other areas, they have room to grow. But in addition to expressing a general desire to receive wisdom from older generations, they are also more likely than others to report both having and being a mentor (see table 13).

Intergenerational relationships have to be more than "Oh, it's so nice when the young people and the old folks get together." Mentoring is not about being cute. It's about getting wise. Gandalf is not cute. Yoda is not cute. (Well, yes. He is. But he's also mystically spooky and can kick Sith butt when he needs to. Plus, he's got nine hundred years of pattern recognition under his tiny belt.) We've got to wade beyond shallow, heartwarming intergenerational fellowship into a deep well of intentional mentoring.

Classic hero stories can be of help to us here.

A mentor from the old school, such as producer Chuck Roven, might start with the question How can I help this kid learn the ropes and pay their dues? And look, that's a perfectly reasonable question. But it's not big enough. It's not heroic.

In a classic hero's journey, a wise mentor arrives to help once the hero has committed to the quest but doesn't yet have what they need to accomplish it. A hero's mentor starts with the question How can I help this hero become who they are meant to be?

Think of Luke Skywalker. He wants to battle the dark side and defeat the Empire—but that kid couldn't find his way out of a paper bag. His real shortcoming, though, is that he doesn't know his limitations. He's committed to the quest and has some obvious talent, but he needs more. He needs humility. Not *humiliation*, but humility—and it takes a wise mentor to

Table 13. Resilient Disciples Embrace Mentoring	Prodigals/ Ex-Christians	Nomads/ Unchurched	Habitual Churchgoers	Resilient Disciples
Percentage who strongly agree with each statement	✖	◉	⛪	◼
I feel valued by the people in my life who are older than me.	24%	26%	37%	65%
I welcome positive criticism from those who are older than me.	29%	30%	35%	60%
I often look to those who are older than me for advice when I need to make difficult decisions.	21%	25%	37%	56%
I have received helpful input from a pastor or church worker about my education.	9%	11%	19%	43%
I became friends with someone at church who has helped guide my professional development.	14%	15%	22%	40%
I have had an adult mentor at church other than the pastor or church staff.	7%	8%	17%	39%
I meet regularly with someone who is a mentor to me.	9%	6%	21%	38%
I meet regularly with someone whom I mentor.	9%	5%	17%	27%

N = 1,514 US 18- to 29-year-olds who grew up as Christians
Source: Barna, February 2018

know the difference. Before Yoda can teach Luke all he knows about using the force, Luke has to become humble. As Yoda explains, "Anger, fear, aggression . . . the dark side of the force are they. Easily they flow, quick to join you in a fight. If once you start down the dark path, forever will it dominate your destiny. Consume you, it will."[4]

Yoda's first task is to help Luke become humble so that he can grow into the hero he is meant to be without getting sidetracked by his darker instincts.

The second question the hero's mentor asks is What do I have to give?

Every mentor has a sacred relic or secret knowledge that can radically change the hero's life. Obi-Wan Kenobi has kept Anakin Skywalker's lightsaber and gives it to Luke. Father Christmas in Narnia has a gift for each of the Pevensie kids, without which they can't win the coming battle against the White Witch. Doc Hudson gives Lightning McQueen the secret to turning on dirt. Fairy Godmother gives Cinderella glass slippers and an unforgettable night on the town.

And so on.

What do you have to give?

You have insights, ideas, tools, and meaningful objects that might not even seem important to you anymore. But for someone just starting out on their journey, these gifts could be life changing. Passing them on is what mentoring is all about.

Vocation in Action

One of David's favorite Christian events is Jubilee, a large conference for college students that takes place in Pittsburgh every February. (They could have picked a better time of year for the wintery climes of western Pennsylvania, just saying.) Despite the bitter cold outside, the presentations, workshops, and booksellers par excellence are, as the kids say, lit. The entire dramatic arc of the event is designed to take students through the creation-fall-redemption-restoration story line of Christianity, with talks and thematic elements helping to build cultural discernment as students progress from Friday's opening session to Sunday's closing bell.

The conference features content from Christian professionals in a variety of fields, literally scores of speakers all sharing with students how to think in a Christian way and how to be a Christian in their particular vocations. It is something to see Christian college students emerging inspired from the sessions, loaded down with books in their arms, talking intently about deep issues of calling and purpose and faith.

When Emily was a junior in high school, David took her to Jubilee. One of her favorite sessions, on physics and faith, was taught by Catherine Crouch, a college professor. In fact, Catherine became a vocational mentor to David's science-minded daughter. Several years later, Emily still consults Catherine about questions surrounding her career plans, aspirations, and concerns and about following Jesus as a disciple called to generate order—a scientist.

Vocational discipleship is a real thing, and we believe that through it the church can be revived. When we read about past revivals, they aren't about society turning to Jesus. They are about the church becoming more faithful to Jesus and more Spirit-led *within* society.

Churches that are serious about vocational discipleship can help young people answer these deep-seated questions:

- Who has God created me to be?
- Does my life matter?
- Am I made for something more?

As a result, the body of Christ will be renewed and revived in digital Babylon.

■■■

If the church has a discipleship problem, then we've got to look for ways to try new things. We see clear evidence that the most resilient young Christians are stronger when we connect discipleship and vocation. They live more integrated lives and understand at a deeper, more essential level that God cares about what they do with their lives. That he has made them to be a masterpiece.

It's a privilege—and a calling in itself—to pay close attention to the sparks of calling in people's lives, especially the lives of those growing up around us.

David's son Zack once asked, "Does God have so much money because he has sold so many Bibles?" A budding entrepreneur, for sure!

Our friend Bill Denzel has taken his son Zion through a number of career and calling assessments during his final years of high school, coaching him along the way to see the bigger picture of God's purposes for his life.

More than just making an ambitions wish list, more than mere competitiveness in the career marketplace, we can help form the next generation of resilient disciples by helping them integrate faith, work, and calling.

Mentoring in Digital Babylon

In order for us to make and to become resilient disciples in our accelerated, complex society, we're going to have to find ways of improving the outcomes of our work together. Sometimes that means creating new models, and other times it means refreshing ancient pathways through modern life. Take mentoring, for example. It is both timeless and timely. Here are a few reflections on how to make mentoring work in our new context.

First, we have to consider what we're trying to convey through the mentoring process. More than ever, it can't just be life lessons and pithy maxims. (Young disciples can get Instagram Scripture memes without our help.) They need wisdom from God's Word.

At one point in his life, Mark wrote down every biblical proverb on an index card and sorted the cards into thematic piles. As he did so, he discovered that each proverb falls into one of seven broad categories. These are the seven marks of a wise person, according to Proverbs:

1. A wise person trusts in God.
2. A wise person walks in healthy relationships.
3. A wise person seeks good counsel.
4. A wise person uses words wisely.
5. A wise person exercises self-control.
6. A wise person manages their resources.
7. Ultimately, a wise person lives in peace.

As a mentor (or parent or young Christian), this list is a good measuring stick for your life and perhaps for that of your young mentee. Here are two big ideas for how to grow these qualities through mentoring friendships.

Three Paths to Wisdom

No matter how we define wisdom, experience is an essential part of acquiring it—which is why we expect people to grow in wisdom as they age (though that isn't always the case). While there is no substitute for experience, we believe a mentor can amplify and accelerate the wisdom their mentee acquires by intentionally leveraging every experience to become a pathway to greater wisdom. This transfer of wisdom between generations is more important than ever because, unless we are intentional, young Christians will be raised by their devices and algorithms rather than by us.

The three main pathways for wisdom within the context of mentoring are reflection, selection, and projection. (One important aspect of wise mentoring is knowing which pathway to take.) Reflection is an opportunity to gain wisdom from what has already happened—from the past. Selection deals with the present and offers chances for a mentee to choose what is wise even as their experience is unfolding. And projection is the future path, where a young disciple can explore what might occur and acquire wisdom for what is to come.

Reflection

Reflection is the pathway of learning from the past. When Jesus asks his disciples, "Who do people say that I am?" he is asking them to reflect on their past experiences among the crowds. The disciples offer their observations, and then Jesus asks, "Who do *you* say that I am?" leading them to answer the question for themselves (see Matt. 16:13–16; Mark 8:27–29; Luke 9:18–20). This is reflection at its very best—and it is a path too rarely taken.

Effective, wisdom-acquiring reflection demands that we stop what we are doing to think about what we have done. It takes time and is often uncomfortable, because we often learn more from our mistakes than our successes. A wise mentor helps their mentee to pause and ask, "What happened? What did I notice about myself and others? Where did I see God at work? Where did I work with or against him? What do these choices mean for who God is calling me to be and what he is calling me to do?"

If pattern recognition is one way to define wisdom, then reflection is the process of identifying patterns from the past so they are recognizable now and in the future.

Selection

If reflection looks back and projection looks ahead, selection is concerned with becoming wise here and now. A good mentor helps their mentee zoom out from the present choice that must be made to see it as part of a larger opportunity for growth and development. This is also when a mentor can share their own experience to advise the choice the young disciple must make—because it *is* possible, and more efficient, to learn from someone else's experiences. As Ben Franklin pithily wrote in his *Poor Richard's Almanack*, "Experience keeps a dear school, but Fools will learn in no other."[5]

Don't let your mentee be a fool, unless they insist on it. Be generous with your experiences. Share your hard-won wisdom. As you guide your mentee through selection, help them notice patterns and predict outcomes. But don't just give them the answer as if you were the answer key in the back of a math book. Show your work. Let them in on the secret of how you got where you are. Then walk with them as they make their own selection— even if it is a bad one.

Projection

Projection is the future pathway, where a mentor helps a mentee "project" into a situation or a relationship they have not yet been in. This might be done by giving them a task, engaging with them in a simulation, role-playing, or creating a story or case study wherein they are able to react with little real-world consequence. Projection is a scrimmage game in which everyone on the field is on the same team, even if they're wearing different jerseys. The athlete builds skills and instincts they couldn't develop any other way, and the coach gets a glimpse, *before* the big game, of how the athlete will play under pressure.

Jesus did this with parables. He projected his listeners into a story and allowed them to interact with it—thereby showing them deeper truth about his kingdom or their own hearts. Or think about the time he fell asleep on a boat during a storm as a carefully crafted simulation to see how his disciples would respond without his physical presence—something they would need to do after his death and resurrection. The disciples panicked, still not convinced they could fully trust the power of God over all forces both natural and supernatural. Jesus's act of calming the wind and the waves was a demonstration of that power, bolstering their trust in him and courage for what was to come.

How can you help your young disciple practice wisdom for the future?

Reciprocal Mentoring

Another critical perspective to embrace when it comes to effective mentoring in digital Babylon is that it can no longer be only a top-down, older-to-younger process. Mentoring today has the potential to shape not only the young disciple but also the older Christ follower. This is especially true when the friendship is mutual rather than hierarchical. The reality is that we in the older generations need knowledge and, yes, wisdom from younger believers, just as they need these from us.

This isn't the case just because young people know more about technology than older adults. The reason is actually much deeper than that. We believe that exiles are not just incidental; they must be *instrumental* in shaping the church (that means all of us) in digital Babylon. Daniel wasn't just marking time in Babylon; God used him to propel his people's faithfulness. Esther wasn't just a sideshow; she literally saved her people. Peter called believers in the early church exiles not because doing so was clever but because God uses exiles. And if that's true (it is), and you are not really all that comfortable with living in exile, maybe you have a thing or two to learn from people who are.

Think about today's young people. They are smart, connected, ambitious, creative, and much more. We are absolutely amazed at how quickly our kids learn things from YouTube and other sources. They are often more informed—and wiser—than we realize. They don't know everything, and we need to learn together to practice reflection, selection, and projection (among other things). But we"d better be ready to admit that we need the next generation of exiles just as much as we hope they sense the need for us.

173

We even have a name for this kind of give-and-take: reciprocal mentoring.

> Reciprocal mentoring opens a free flow of wisdom from one generation to the next and back again.
>
> It offers older adults the chance to learn new tools and frameworks.
>
> It projects mentors into new situations that require new or adapted patterns.
>
> It helps older generations develop empathy and new insights into the experiences of the young.
>
> It gives us tools to map the contours of a social landscape that is no longer "Christian."
>
> It generates courage to have difficult conversations with people we disagree with.
>
> It helps us to lead with love in our relationships with those inside and outside the church.
>
> It offers a framework and a passion for engaging the world.
>
> It shines a light on a mentor's box so they can think outside of it.
>
> It keeps the mentor humble so they can continue their own hero's journey.

A relationship of reciprocal mentoring isn't quick and clean. Toes will be stepped on. Egos will be wounded. Crosses will be taken up. But:

> If any of you wants to be my follower, you must give up your own way, take up your cross, and follow me. If you try to hang on to your life, you will lose it. But if you give up your life for my sake, you will save it. (Matt. 16:24–25)

Curb Entitlement and Self-Centered Tendencies by Engaging in Countercultural Mission

Engaging in countercultural mission means living as a faithful presence by trusting God's power and living differently from cultural norms.

A walk in the woods is good for the soul. For the Kinnamans, hiking the national parks is worshiping in cathedrals of God's making.

It's the spring of 2016, and the five of us are heading down into the Grand Canyon—very down. Starting from the south rim, the trip is about ten miles one way, all downhill, to Phantom Ranch. We are planning to camp at the bottom. Hikers descend nearly forty-five hundred feet, almost a mile, down.

Then there's the ten miles back. We not-so-intrepid explorers must *ascend* that forty-five hundred feet back up.

It's not called the *Grand* Canyon for nothing.

Emily, our oldest daughter, forgot to pack a jacket (I'm not bitter), and so we are doing some last-minute shopping at the Grand Canyon Lodge. A woman in her midtwenties who works at the store helps us find the right merchandise. As she does, I notice she's limping.

Sometimes Barna research pops into my head at weird times, and this moment, shopping for a jacket, is one of them. As the clerk shows us overpriced jackets (we are far from the places where provisions are available at reasonable prices), I visualize the statistic that 52 percent of adults think praying out loud in public for a stranger is extremist.

Despite the risk of social awkwardness, I feel compelled to offer to pray for her.

"Thanks for helping us find the right size," I say and then, after a pause in which I calculate the pros and cons, offer tentatively, "Hey, I notice you're limping. You okay?"

"No, my leg is really sore. I went on a long hike yesterday and hurt it."

"Bummer."

"I sort of *had* to come into work today."

I nod, imagining a boss she's trying to appease and bills she has to pay. "I know this may sound a little strange, but would you mind if I pray with you—for your leg?" I ask with as much nonaggressive conviction as I can muster.

She looks at me with the kind of head tilt that dogs do, and I can tell she's doing a mental calculation similar to the one I just performed. I can also feel the what-are-you-doing-Dad stare from my then-twelve-year-old son, Zack, standing beside me.

"Sure, that'd be okay with me," she says with a sincere smile. I glance down at Zack, who's looking at me with emoji-wide blue eyes.

"Cool, let's pray," I say and bow my head just enough. "God in heaven, would you please help my new friend Shannon to feel better? Her leg is causing her a lot of pain, and we know you can heal people. So I am asking you to heal her and to take away her pain so she can work today. I pray this in Jesus's name, amen."

I open my eyes just before she does. She smiles again and thanks me. "Sure, no problem, you're welcome"—those kinds of words come out. Nothing seems to have miraculously happened at that moment, but she seems grateful.

As we walk away, Zack half whispers, "Dad, we really believe this stuff, don't we?"

On a Mission from God

Thinking back to that experience, I can't help but believe that Christianity is meant to be at odds with purposeless, going-through-the-motions life. (I also can't help but remember how sore my calf muscles were after the hike, but that's another story.) Although most people think praying for a stranger in public is religious extremism, we have an obligation and an opportunity as Christians to be the *right kind of extreme*.

Keep Christianity weird.

This leads us to the fifth and final practice for raising resilient young disciples: engaging in God's countercultural mission. Let's break this down a bit. The idea of being "countercultural" generates many images, from eating vegan to composting to tie-dye to bell-bottoms. The way we're using the word, countercultural is a way of life in Jesus that runs against the grain of the world. This connects back to our original definition of discipleship, covered in an earlier chapter: to develop Jesus followers who are resiliently faithful in the face of cultural coercion and who live a vibrant life in the Spirit.

The Christian community, when it is most faithful, runs contrary to and is distinct from the systems and structures of power, sexuality, and money, among many other things. We are called to be a counterculture for the common good.[1] Scripture says, "Don't copy the behavior and customs of this world, but let God transform you into a new person by changing the way you think" (Rom. 12:2). This is at the heart of being countercultural.

The word *mission* calls to mind everything from impossible exploits (Tom Cruise jumping out of an airplane) to visiting five stores to find the right pair of shoes. In the realm of faith, we might picture a missionary working in dusty, far-off places of the earth. But the idea of mission we're conveying here is that God is powerful, active, and intentional, and he wants his followers to play a part in redeeming people and restoring the world to himself. Biblically speaking, this includes a wide range of aspirations, including serving others, caring for creation, receiving God's blessing in order to bless others, and seeking to save the lost in Jesus's name.

That God chooses to work his mission in part through his people is astounding. The God of the universe wants us to be part of his mission! He doesn't need us to do his work, but we have the privilege of joining with him, the master craftsman, in the mission to reconcile the world to himself. Why does he want us to join in?

Have you ever done something you really love to do *with someone*, maybe one of your kids? Hiking is fun. Hiking with my family is even more enjoyable. God shares his grand mission with us—and wants us to live out his mission with others too—because he loves to love *with us.*

We now have the building blocks to further define the fifth practice of resilient discipleship:

> Engaging in countercultural mission means living
> as a faithful presence[2] by trusting God's power
> and living differently from cultural norms.

This sounds awesome! However, it is especially hard, uphill, soul-shaping work for people in exile. It makes the Grand Canyon look like a walk in the park.

Resilient and Resolute

This fifth practice represents the most elusive of the five. We looked at more than a dozen factor combinations for how best to understand it. Our team kept sifting through threads of evidence and data, searching for how to best isolate and identify the factors at work. Analysts looked first at outward-facing elements, factors that show young disciples caring about Christianity being expressed *for outsiders,* not just for those already inside the tent. In the end, we landed on the idea that this factor could best be described as a sense of mission for the cause of Christ in the world—and a resolute orientation toward walking against the grain of culture. This is not easy, but the research shows that young resilient disciples are doing just this (see table 14).

How does countercultural mission relate to the other practices we have been exploring in *Faith for Exiles*? Intimacy with

Jesus is the deep source of our identity here on earth and in eternity. Cultural discernment involves the life of the mind and the robust perspectives we must cultivate together in order to think Christianly about ourselves and the world. Meaningful relationships are about devotion to other believers who shape us to become more like Christ. Vocational discipleship relates to personal calling and finding what God has made each of us to do. Countercultural mission is the outward-facing expression of all the other practices—what we do together as the body of Christ for the sake of the world. It is about the people of God resolving to be on mission together to influence the world toward God's good, original intentions.

In the research among resilients, we found some startling patterns.

Table 14. **Resilient Disciples Have a Strong Sense of Mission** *Percentage who strongly agree with each statement*	Prodigals/ Ex-Christians	Nomads/ Unchurched	Habitual Churchgoers	Resilient Disciples
I want others to see Jesus reflected in me through my words and actions.	11%	29%	50%	90%
I, personally, have a responsibility to tell others about my religious beliefs.	7%	11%	34%	76%
I am excited by the mission of the church in today's world.	5%	8%	32%	67%
A major part of my purpose in life is to serve others.	21%	20%	35%	66%

N = 1,514 US 18- to 29-year-olds who grew up as Christians
Source: Barna, February 2018

- *Resilient disciples live with a sense of mission.* Among more than forty statements and factors in the category of countercultural mission, the most commonly embraced among resilient disciples is "I want others to see Jesus reflected in me through my words and actions." Nine out of ten resilients strongly agree. Three-quarters strongly feel that "I, personally, have a responsibility to tell others about my religious beliefs," and two-thirds are "excited by the mission of the church in today's world."

- *Resilient disciples express strong belief in the reality of God's work in the world.* An aspect of this is their firm conviction about the supernatural dimension of life. The vast majority of resilients believe that "miracles really happen in our world today" (including that "Jesus is able to heal people today"), that "the Holy Spirit leads me each day," and that Christians face a "real spiritual adversary called the devil." More than four out of five resilients strongly believe the second coming of Jesus will happen one day.

- *Resilient disciples feel (mostly) supported by their churches when it comes to living out their faith.* We examined more than twenty factors of countercultural mission that churches help to instill in the next generation, the most common of which is "courage to live my faith in public." However, there are many ways resilients suggest they could be better supported by their churches, as we'll see later in this chapter.

- *Resilient disciples often have more confidence in what they believe than clarity about how to express those convictions.* This is the one area in which resilient disciples show the most room for growth and the most inconsistent sense of purpose. They often express confidence in their beliefs, such as the idea of God's design for sexuality. However, they are more likely to struggle with knowing how to have difficult conversations with peers who believe differently.

- *Resilient disciples want to serve.* Resilients show major differences from others in their aspiration to help people, quite apart from any spiritual prompting. Even when asked to verify a straightforward, spiritually neutral statement, "A major part of my purpose in life is to serve others," two-thirds strongly agree. That compares to just one-third of other churchgoers and only one-fifth of nomads and prodigals.

Resilients exhibit a powerful, resolute commitment to serving and sacrificing for others. These are the kinds of young people we want to produce—and the kind of people we want to be! However, this is certainly not the norm—and it is not how most people perceive young adults.

Entitled and Self-Centered

When you think about Millennials—and about the next, next generation, Gen Z—what are some of the words or phrases that come to mind? David routinely asks this question when speaking in front of audiences of pastors and Christian workers. Here's a sample of words offered by a group of pastors and church leaders in Sacramento. (Seriously, this is based on a transcript from that day.)

selfish

lost

hipsters

tech savvy

flakes

gamers

entitled

foodies

self-absorbed

lazy

incredibly good looking (That came from—you guessed
  it—a Millennial.)

courageous (This was the first genuinely positive comment
  from any of the older adults in the room. As you can see,
  it broke open a different direction.)

passionate

sincere

hopeful

pressured

unparented

overparented

Surely you have heard some of these negative Millennial stereotypes. By the way, history records many instances—one even shows up in ancient Athens—of older people complaining about the next generation. This is an age-old problem; we worry about our youth.

But in our particular moment—in digital Babylon—it's interesting that so many Boomers and Elders are complaining about Millennials. Here's our question: Who raised the Millennials? How is it that the people who raised them are the ones complaining most vociferously? We grumble about handing out participation trophies, but who bought those trophies and handed them out?

Disparate life experiences lead generations to dismiss and devalue one another. But the church must be the place we give no quarter to that destructive thinking. We need one another to get on with our mission.

Still, many of us sense something in the air, something that feeds entitlement and self-absorption.

Curbing Entitlement

Any parent will say they want to avoid raising entitled kids. But this is almost like swearing we will never be like our parents: what we resist persists. It becomes a self-fulfilling prophecy. Avoiding entitlement is difficult when we tend to make little idols out of our kids. Once a neighbor observed that Zack Kinnaman, a little boy at the time, was essentially the prince of the house. David felt pretty defensive at the time. But the truth hurts.

We've just joked about participation trophies, but there is some truth to the entitlements that come when we create everyone-deserves-to-be-acknowledged schools and everyone-is-awesome workplaces. When it comes to finding their destiny, we feed the next generation all sorts of myths about being able to achieve whatever they want, about becoming anything they can dream, about finding what their hearts desire most. Most twentysomethings expect to have attained their dream job within the next five years, but only half as many say they have clear goals for how they're going to get there.

Part of the reason older adults chafe at their interactions with younger adults and teens is that they genuinely can't relate. I (David) always felt inadequate when I worked for George Barna, like he was going to find out what a poser I really was. For *years*, I felt that way. One of my Millennial staff, only six months on the job, told me she felt like her career had plateaued. Another twentysomething team member came out of a client presentation and announced, "I pretty much nailed that, right?!" I couldn't even imagine having that kind of confidence when I was their age.

A legendary music producer, musician, and songwriter once commiserated, "These Millennials come into my studio and treat me like I am their peer, not just in terms of age but in terms of experience and accomplishments. It's so rare to find a good musician or singer these days who doesn't think they *deserve* to be a star." Welcome to the YouTube era and the expectation of making it. Like, now.

A thirty-year veteran of the airlines recently observed that what's different about fliers today is that "everyone thinks they deserve the royal treatment." Sure, many Millennials are entitled. But perhaps they are a product of their environment. They are children of entitled parents who can't help but spoil their beautiful, amazing kids.

As Christians—whatever our age—we have to practice a countercultural mission on this level. We have to curb our sense of entitlement. We have to fight the zeitgeist when it sneaks in like an unseen digital cookie on our web browser. Being countercultural means being dead set against entitlement in our lives. And to do that, we've got to work to develop the muscles of sacrifice and service. The Scriptures point the way. We must decrease so that Jesus can increase (John 3:30). The first shall be last, and the last shall be first (Matt. 20:16). Blessed are the meek, for they will inherit the earth (Matt. 5:5).

Turning from Self-Centeredness

In addition to swelling problems of entitlement, society is plagued by self-centeredness. These problems ride together, like a bank robber and a getaway driver. Jean Twenge, whom we mentioned earlier, has written extensively about the narcissism epidemic.[3] There's actually solid social research showing that a higher proportion of people in our society today display characteristics of narcissistic behavior compared to people in the past. (How cool is it that social scientists can measure something like narcissism? Long live the geeks!) Twenge believes this is tied, at least in part, to pervasive screen use. The objects themselves do not make us self-centered but the way we use them does. These tools create a my-sized experience all day, every day.

The signs of self-centered, self-indulgent, me-first mindsets are all around us. They are often disguised as "the pursuit of happiness." David's dad, Gary Kinnaman, who served as a pastor for decades in Phoenix, was once asked by a woman who wanted to get divorced and remarried, "But the Bible says God wants me to be happy, right?" When we survey the leading edge of Gen Z, we find that 51 percent of teens today say their top goal for life is happiness.

Self-centeredness can also masquerade as society-wide perspectives, such as the belief held by the vast majority of Americans that people can believe whatever they want as long as those beliefs don't harm anyone. And as we've discussed, most adults say a person finds their truest self by looking *inside*. Neither of these ideas really work.

Now, before we cast all the blame for self-centered behavior on everyone else, we should also look close to home. We can spot self-centered tendencies in the pulpit and in Christian ministries. There are broken human beings there, so of course that's true. In our efforts to live a countercultural mission, however, we must diagnose and fix self-centeredness in our churches. Here are a few things to ponder.

- We find evidence that many—though certainly not all— pastors struggle to exhibit intellectual humility. For instance, they think they are more right more often than the general population.
- Many pastors admit they don't enjoy developing younger leaders—but ensuring the transfer of leadership to the next generation is a requirement, not a choice.
- There's good reason to believe that thousands of pastors in the US are staying in their posts too long, blockading many able and willing emerging leaders. One factor is that they are financially unable to retire. But even if that's true, they are constraining the pipeline for future pastors.
- Despite overwhelming evidence showing that discipleship is about developing the whole person and involves more than what happens on Sunday mornings from the pulpit, most pastors admit they love to preach and teach but don't really love the people development or pastoral side of leading a church.
- Most church leader conferences and ministry magazines showcase people and models that attract large numbers of attendees, but less attention is given to leaders who are engaging in serving and sacrificing on behalf of their communities.

The point here isn't to rag on pastors but to suggest that, in order for the church to engage in healthy mission today, we need strong leaders who aren't focused on themselves—who embody the countercultural, kingdom way of deflecting attention to Jesus. This may seem counterintuitive, but we need more leaders who accomplish less in the limelight and more behind the scenes to shape the hearts, minds, and souls of the next generation. We can't power our way to kingdom impact. It just doesn't work that way.

At the same time, this is a call for all of us—leader and laity, younger and older, child, parent, and grandparent. In digital Babylon—in the era of YouTube, Twitter, self-promotion, and the humble brag—we must learn to put self aside. This is the countercultural way of Jesus.

What will it take to rid us of our self-centered ways? It will require the same kinds of practices that help to check entitlement: service, sacrifice, silence, solitude, letting go of control, thinking less about ourselves, and so on. It will mean having an engaged heart toward one another and for the sake of others. One of the many remarkable facts about the Bible is that the Old Testament ends, as it turns to the story of Jesus, by saying that God will turn the hearts of the fathers toward their children and the hearts of the children toward their fathers.

Having a shared mission is one way of thinking about ourselves less.

God's People in Exile

In one of the most beautiful passages of the Bible, the prophet Jeremiah predicts the coming exile. His powerful, poetic language doesn't persuade all his hearers. Not everyone considers his warnings to be accurate; many suspect Jeremiah of taking crazy pills. Understandably, they don't want to leave their comfortable way of life in Jerusalem.

But Jeremiah proves to be right, and his prophecy offers practical insights about living as God's people in exile. Here are some of the insights Jeremiah offers (see Jer. 29), set alongside the ways Daniel and other exiles exemplify these principles of countercultural mission.

- *Exiles should make prayer a mission.* Jeremiah encourages his readers to pray for the peace and prosperity of the city where God has sent them into exile. Later, Daniel's missional prayers provide the platform for his rise to prominence, his prescient service to multiple kings, and the political pressure he faces in his final years.

- *Exiles should be faithful and holy.* A clear theme of the life and times of exiles is the need for faithfulness to God and holiness. Exile comes along partly because the people of God lose the map to holiness. That is a recurring theme in the Old Testament, and Jeremiah certainly echoes this idea: when God's people lose their distinctive, set-apart way of life, times of purifying must come. In addition, the way of spiritual growth and cultural impact in exile is through the pursuit of holiness. First Peter 1:17 advises, "If you call on him as Father who judges impartially according to each one's deeds, conduct yourselves with fear throughout the time of your exile" (ESV). Other translations use the phrase "reverent fear" to describe the posture of faithful exiles.

- *Exiles should be fruitful.* Jeremiah's prophecy implores the people to plant trees and gardens, to build homes

189

and households, to marry and have children. Jeremiah's notion that exiles should "plan to stay" is exactly the opposite message these men and women want to hear. Who wouldn't want to return home? But the calling of exiles is to form a generative community that blesses others.

- *Exiles should live for the sake of others.* Part of their "fruitful" calling is to bless others, even (and sometimes especially) nonbelievers. Jeremiah makes an argument for mutuality: seeking Babylon's welfare will benefit the Babylonians *and* the exiles. Many other exiles play out this story line too. The nations are blessed through Abraham. The Egyptians and many more are saved by the prudence of Joseph. Daniel advocates to save the lives of pagan philosophers. Peter's writings show that the church—even when being persecuted—ought to pray for those in power.

- *Exiles must be wary, realistic, and also hopeful.* Just as a dad might give special instructions to his college-bound child, Jeremiah warns exiles not to be tricked. Do not listen to false prophets or fortune-tellers! A certain be-on-your-guard mind-set undergirds life in exile. As a counterbalance to wariness, Jeremiah provides rich, textured hope in one of the most-quoted verses in all the Bible: "'For I know the plans I have for you,' says the LORD. 'They are plans for good and not for disaster, to give you a future and a hope'" (Jer. 29:11).

- *Exiles should take epic risks to say and do what is right.* An undercurrent of Jeremiah's life is that he is willing to tell wildly uncomfortable, unpopular truths to the Hebrew people, even when doing so could cost him his life. Exiles should take these kinds of risks because they believe in the rightness of God's cause. Esther's life demonstrates this principle in spades: she risks her own life for the salvation of the Hebrew people.

- *Exiles should realize that God is at work for good, even in exile.* Jeremiah's famous command begins with the idea that God himself is giving the instructions. Later, Daniel offers clear witness to this idea in his life but also specifically when he tells Nebuchadnezzar, "God is sovereign over the kingdoms of men, and he gives them to whom he wishes" (Dan. 4:17). In the New Testament, the same principle rings out: we don't have to fear God being absent; he shows up even (and sometimes especially) when his people are in the minority.
- *Exiles must find their home in God.* Jeremiah writes on behalf of a God who is present and who desires access to human hearts: "In those days when you pray, I will listen. If you look for me wholeheartedly, you will find me. I will be found by you" (Jer. 29:12–14). Peter's letter to the "exiles" under the oppression of Babylon (Rome) is designed to help them find their identity in Jesus and what he has done for them.

The point of all this? To remind us who follow Jesus that being in exile is a high and ultimately rewarding calling. There is beauty in exile. To live as God's people, to follow his Son through the power of his Spirit, requires us to choose—going along just won't do. The conditions of exile invite us each day to choose whom we will serve.

And in spite of the intense pressures coming at Christians in our post-Christian context, right now, today, at this very moment, millions of young resilient disciples are making their choice. Their lives demonstrate a firm and countercultural trust that God is on the move. Young Christians are coming to grips with how to live as God's people, embracing the power of exile (see table 15).

Here's where things get tricky: the Christian community—inlcuding parents, church leaders, and other well-meaning stakeholders—sometimes works at cross-purposes with regard to young disciples' participation in countercultural mission. We try to keep them insulated. We helicopter-parent them. We imagine that safety and security are kingdom values. We want them to change the world around them, but only at a reasonable distance. We like the *idea* of countercultural mission, but in practice, here in exile, it's kind of terrifying. Living faithfully in Jerusalem, when everything is neat and predictable, is a different animal from faithfulness in Babylon. Too many of our ministry efforts prepare people for a world that doesn't exist, undercutting our witness and passing flimsy faith to the next generation. Because, honestly, we are scared.

Take Courage

Courage is among the most important virtues we can cultivate in digital Babylon. Acknowledging our fear and trusting God in spite of it are job one. Courage helps to empower our definition of discipleship: to develop Jesus followers who are resiliently faithful in the face of cultural coercion and who live a vibrant life in the Spirit. Without courage, we'll be unable to live distinctly from the inexorable push and pull of culture. Without courage, we won't think and live differently from the norm. Without courage, we'll use screens the way everyone

Table 15. How Churches Contribute to Countercultural Mission

Which of the following, if any, do you regularly experience in your church, parish, or faith community? Please mark any that apply. And if none apply, please feel free to mark that.

	Resilient Disciples
Building Courage and Conversational Readiness	
Courage to live my faith in public.	73%
Courage to tell others about what I believe.	64%
Wisdom for living with people who believe differently from me.	56%
Preparation for having difficult conversations with others.	49%
Stoking Compassion	
I better understand the needs of the poor.	65%
I had the opportunity to serve the poor in my community.	58%
I have found a cause or issue that I'm passionate about.	53%
I better understand what is happening for the poor globally.	50%
I better understand social justice.	44%
I better understand the needs of marginalized people.	37%
Giving Real Opportunities to Contribute	
I am given real chances to contribute to my church.	73%
I have learned what it feels like to be part of a team.	57%
I have access to leadership training for ministry through my church.	48%
Preparing a Countercultural Response	
Wisdom for how to live faithfully in a secular world.	70%
Wisdom for how to live differently from the culture.	61%
Prayer specifically for the challenges of living faithfully in a post-Christian culture.	55%
Help with living wisely when it comes to sex and sexuality.	52%
Modeling Faithfulness	
I have been inspired to live generously based on the example of people at my church.	61%
I have been inspired to be a leader based on the example of someone at my church.	51%
I have been inspired to be a missionary based on the example of someone else.	36%

N = 1,178 US 18- to 29-year-olds who grew up as Christians
Source: Barna, February 2018

else does. Without courage, we won't stand up for the right things at the right time.

Resilient disciples take courage from their participation in church. Seven out of ten say that their churches help them to find "courage to live my faith in public" and "wisdom for how to live faithfully in a secular world." Courage doesn't just happen; it has to be taught and reinforced. Joshua continually had to be reminded—by God himself, mind you—to be strong and courageous. Jesus's own words remind us that we will experience troubles in this world but to "take heart, because [he has] overcome the world" (John 16:33).

Don't Put Safety First

Barna has found undeniable evidence that parents of many teenagers are highly motivated by a desire for their safety.[4] This is more than just wanting for them a place free from, say, the possibility of sexual misconduct. Parents *and* students should want that kind of safety. But the safety some parents want is far beyond what is kingdom minded. Many Millennials who dropped out of church tell us that among their chief reasons was feeling their church was overprotective, keeping them insulated from seeing and experiencing the real world.

Churches *should* offer safe refuge and respite from the world; disciples in exile want and need sanctuary and rest from the pressures of accelerated culture.[5] Yet—and this is a big yet—exile is not safe. God's mission is not safe. Participating in God's countercultural mission in exile is certainly not safe—and we do young disciples zero favors by putting safety first. We can be a source of comfort, strength, and like-minded community for Jesus followers in digital Babylon *and* equip them for fruitful, missional living in exile.

The two of us have recently been learning this uncomfortable lesson, not just because we have kids in college but also because they elected to attend highly secular schools (UC Berkeley and Parsons School of Design) in highly post-Christian cities (San Francisco and New York City). If safety came first, Emily and Skye would be at home right now. But because we want our kids to become ever more resilient, safety has gotten bumped from the top of the list.

Our friends John and Beth Fankhauser left their cushy life in Southern California to serve as medical missionaries in Liberia. They took their children, Josh, Bethany, and Bekah, with them to Africa, and they were all there when the Ebola crisis broke out. They were careful, of course, but the false notion of safety didn't come first in their decision to go.

The lesson of faithfulness in exile? Life isn't going to be safe, parents. Put mission first.

Prepare for Difficult Conversations

If courage is among the most essential virtues, the ability to engage in difficult conversations is among the most critical *practical* skills for life in digital Babylon. We live in a world of openly stated differences and religious pluralism, much like the exiles of the Bible did. Today's young Christians live and relate in a difficult conversational landscape: more diversity religiously, more empowered atheism, more insulating tribalism, more social media, more pontificating, less listening.

On the positive side of the ledger, resilient disciples show the right kind of instincts when it comes to difficult conversations. Two-thirds say that their churches give them "courage to tell others what I believe." They are more likely than their peers to say they are interested in learning about the views of others, even if those views are contrary to their own. This is great, because we need young people who aren't frightened by the big, bad world of ideas around them. They are also more likely than their peers to say that it is okay to tell someone you disagree with their opinion or point of view, which is rare in a time of anxiety-producing political correctness.

However, even resilients need help preparing for difficult conversations. Many say that their churches have left them unprepared to have difficult conversations. Also, nearly half agree that one should not criticize someone else's life choices— a belief that is inconsistent with countercultural mission because God calls all Christians to bear witness to the truth in Jesus. When others are headed full speed toward destructive dead ends, questioning their life choices is not the worst thing one can do.

When Gabe Lyons and David released *Good Faith*, a book designed to help equip people for difficult conversations, we heard from many young Christians who felt overwhelmed by the prospect of expressing their convictions with love in our divisive culture. They didn't want to come across as bigoted or out of touch. For us, this was more evidence that helping people know what they believe and how to express themselves to others in a spirit of love and respect is an area where the church must dramatically improve its effectiveness.

Embody a Godly Sexual Ethic

Sex and sexuality are some of the most complicated issues humans have to sort out—and they often serve up complicated and heart-wrenching conversations. Resilient disciples feel the tension of being countercultural in this area.

While most of society agrees that "any kind of sexual expression between consenting adults is acceptable," resilients don't go along with this idea. When asked if they agree or disagree with the statement "Sex is designed by God to be between a man and a woman in marriage," the vast majority of resilient disciples strongly agree (81 percent), starkly contrasting with their peers. Forty-six percent of habituals, 26 percent of nomads, and 12 percent of prodigals embrace this biblically traditional view of sexuality. Resilient disciples *disagree* that Christianity's traditional sexual ethics are unrealistic by a three to one margin (74 percent to 26 percent). Habituals are split in agreement versus disagreement (48 percent to 53 percent). The vast majority of nomads and prodigals agree that Christianity's sexual ethics are unrealistic today.

Resilients display truly different values when it comes to sex. This is remarkable, given all that's stacked against them—the hypersexualized context of digital Babylon and the increasing softening of churches' convictions regarding sexuality—and these young Christians should be commended for their solid beliefs. Still, only half of resilients say that their churches have provided them with help for "living wisely when it comes to sex and sexuality." This number is not bad, but it ought to be higher, especially since responding well to the anything-goes sexuality of our day is deeply connected to resilience.

The most effective churches we've come across take young people through thoughtful, intentional content on sex and sexuality and are careful not to rely merely on Sunday morning sermons to do the heavy lifting on such intense topics. They ask a lot of their young people (reading books and listening to talks and respectfully listening to those they disagree with) and work hard to make a sexual ethic more than skin deep, more than a list of theoretical dos and don'ts. Why? Because living a countercultural ethic when it comes to sex and sexuality is essential to faithful and fruitful mission today.

Lead with Love

In digital Babylon, people come together from a variety of experiences, perspectives, and tribes. Consequently, there is no mainstream way of seeing and interpreting the world, and exiles have to work out friendships and relationships in a context different from that of previous generations. Young resilients want to learn to be friends across differences. They value diversity. They don't want to vote people off the island.

Earlier in *Faith for Exiles*, we talked about Christian-to-Christian relationships because these are central to our formation as believers. In exile, however, this is not the only kind of relationship young people experience. Young Christians live in a profoundly pluralistic culture—religiously, culturally, in every way. Difference abounds.

Millennial and Gen Z Christians are trying to figure out how to navigate this culture. They experience empathy for people not like themselves. This is a good and godly instinct. Paul wrote that he became all things to all people so that he might win some to Christ (1 Cor. 9:21–22). He appealed to his Greek hearers by talking about the "Unknown God" (Acts 17:22–23). He advised his readers to have "gracious and attractive" conversations with nonbelievers (Col. 4:6). He went so far as to say that the sexual ethics of Christianity shouldn't be applied to non-Christians (1 Cor. 5:9–13).

Exiles live faithfully on mission by leading with love, building empathy, seeing people for who they are, and acknowledging the image of God in them.

In our experience, too often Christians put up unhelpful walls and barriers that prevent the forward movement of the gospel. Christians can't hang out with LGBTQ people, some might say. Christians shouldn't agree with political liberals. Or maybe with political conservatives. We have heard Christians poke fun at the idea of trigger warnings and safe spaces, which is ironic because Christians have many words that trigger their own fear and loathing. Here in digital Babylon, the expression of mercy and forgiveness toward others is as rare as ever, and maybe more. (Have you seen how ugly things can get on Twitter and Facebook?)

Exiles have both a responsibility and an opportunity to participate in God's mission, even in the relational tension of our times. To be in but not of. To express God's love through Jesus's work on the cross to a hurting and waiting world, regardless of political affiliation, sexual orientation, or religious affiliation.

Work Together for the Sake of Others

Another set of mission-related outcomes relates to working with other Christians to bless others, especially those in need. For example, resilient disciples say that their churches play a significant role in helping them understand the needs of the poor both locally and globally and in giving them real opportunities to serve the poor. They truly feel they are part of a serving team. The statement "I am given real chances to contribute to my church" is endorsed by 73 percent of resilients. A majority of resilient disciples say that they have learned "what it feels like to be part of a team" by virtue of their church engagement. And almost half say that they "have access to leadership training for ministry through my church"—a result that is significantly higher among resilients than among any other group. There is still room for improvement among churches regarding these factors, but countercultural mission is formed in community.

Some resilient disciples also told us they experience inspiration to live generously (61 percent), to be a leader (51 percent), and to be a missionary (36 percent) based on the example of someone in their churches. This is a cool trio of findings! The faithfulness of other (usually older) Christians models the way of Christian mission in the world. These outcomes are more than twice as likely among resilient disciples than among habitual churchgoers and many times more likely than among nomads and prodigals.

Our shared mission together propels the next generation.

Make a Difference

If you've been tracking along, you've probably noticed that each of the five practices correspond to existential questions every human being asks. Throughout this book, we've tried to build the case that following Jesus offers answers to the deepest longings of our hearts.

We suggest that countercultural mission addresses essential questions about legacy and significance.

- Can I make a difference?
- What really matters?
- What counts for a life well lived?

Today's emerging generations, like all generations, desire to do something that really matters, something that lasts. Entitlement, narcissism, self-centeredness, consumerism all act as Hungry, Hungry Hippos, gobbling up our time, attention, and compassion. Digital Babylon steals away our precious time for vain and frivolous things. Flimsy, Brand-Jesus Christianity doesn't have a chance.

But by participating in Jesus's countercultural mission in the world, we can make a difference. We can carve out a life well lived, for the sake of others.

- We can sacrifice of ourselves.
- We can put aside selfish ambition.
- We can pray for the peace and prosperity of our cities.
- We can experience Jesus doing miracles.
- We can trust God's power and live differently from cultural norms.

Reality is both physical and spiritual, and since Jesus has been given authority over all things, we participate with him as restorers in both the physical and the spiritual dimensions of life. We do good to and in the world. We bless others. Jesus's mission to seek and save the lost, to set the captives free, inspires. It matters. It lasts.

■ ■ ■

About the time David released the book *You Lost Me*, he came across the book *Kisses from Katie*, which describes the missionary journey of Katie Davis (now Katie Davis Majors). At eighteen years of age, she was the senior class president and homecoming queen in her Nashville high school. But when she decided to go on a mission trip instead of attending college, she disappointed her parents and teachers, lost most of her friends, and broke up with the love of her life. None of that stopped her. After graduation, she headed to Uganda, where she couldn't speak the language and knew only one other person.

After that short mission trip, she found herself so moved by the people in Uganda that she knew she had to return. When she did, she began the process of adopting thirteen Ugandan orphans. And there she lived as a single woman, facing rough conditions, depending entirely on God to provide for the needs of her and her kids. And she found in her life of service a deep joy. Talk about an extremist!

Katie went on to form Amazima Ministries, an organization that matches donors with orphaned children to pay for schooling, school supplies, food, minor medical care, and spiritual encouragement.

Why? Why would someone do something so not normal? Why would she go against the cultural grain, sacrificing a bright and promising future?

Because Katie is a resilient disciple of Christ. Because participation in God's countercultural mission is a life well lived.

■ ■ ■

David's good friend Dudley Chancey is a youth ministry practitioner and professor who also runs projects to help the poor in Honduras. He is another resilient disciple living out his faith in exile, someone dedicated to countercultural mission. The stories he tells of serving children and taking Americans on his adventures bring a lump to my throat. Dudley inspires me, and as I finish up the writing on this manuscript, I've got a trip to Honduras coming up with Dudley in about a month. I'll be taking my kids, Zack and Annika, to work alongside me, helping in whatever ways Dudley has in mind. I'm picturing the various projects we'll work on and the look on Zack's face when he sees all the good Dudley and his crew are doing.

At some point on the trip home to California, I like to imagine leaning close to my son and whispering, "See, Zack? We really believe this stuff!"

What's Next

Finding Hope in Exiles

For years, the two of us have advocated for the next generation of believers. We've tried to warm up older leaders to the fact that Millennials, and now Gen Z, aren't going to ruin the world or the church. Sure, there will be frustrations between generations along the way, but young adults and teens today are smart, connected, funny, creative, genuine, ambitious, and optimistic. They are a generation of hope. We, the Christian community, would do well to put our confidence in them.

We've spent the last few years researching and listening to young resilient disciples across the country, who are Bible-minded, mission-driven, Jesus-centered people. We come away from this project with massive respect and love for young Jesus followers, these faithful exiles. Yes, they are young and make mistakes. But we were young once too. We made, and continue to make, mistakes by the truckload.

The next generation of resilient Christians face uncertain times. The pressures of digital Babylon are brutally dehumanizing and often antithetical to faith. They deeply feel the dizzying effects of the screen era. They talk about the bittersweet experience of being faithful in exile, their frustrations and disappointments and concerns—often with the church. They, like any group of young leaders who face stiff headwinds, realize their task won't be easy. Society is confusing, and the Christian community is complicated.

Yet they long to serve and to lead the church into the next decades. We do well to place our hope in them. Our ultimate hope is in the resurrected Christ and his promise of new life. Raising resilient disciples and then trusting the church to their care is an exercise in trusting the Lord.

For many of us, balancing realism and hope is a tall task.

■■■

David's father, Gary Kinnaman, spent nearly thirty years pastoring a church in Phoenix, Arizona. He planted the church in the suburb of Mesa in the mid-1980s and remained there until 2008. The church grew every year under his leadership, reaching weekly attendance of more than five thousand people. But then came several years of declining attendance and giving, so he decided to move along to the next assignment God had for him. He did so in his late fifties, much earlier than most successful leaders with a good salary and job security would think to do.

My dad has always been kingdom minded. For instance, he took very much to heart the idea that the years of decline weren't his "fault," that the people of God were not his sole responsibility. But he also took to heart the knowledge that the years of incredible growth were not his doing, so he took no credit for the great things God had done. Being realistic about the ups and downs of ministry allowed my dad to give God the glory.

I asked him recently to describe his decision to step aside. There were many reasons, but two interesting parts of his story are relevant. First, he said I had told him that I couldn't think of any examples, based on Barna research, of church decline that were turned around by the current pastor. I have no memory of this conversation, but it shows how the Holy Spirit was active in his life, helping him to look squarely and realistically at what might work.

Second, he read a book by Reggie McNeal called *The Present Future: Six Tough Questions for the Church*. In recounting the impact of the book, he told me, "I read it on a long flight from Australia, so I had a chance to sort of marinate in what it was saying. And I sat there thinking, *I don't really have answers to what Reggie is raising. I don't think I have the skills in my leadership to lead the church through these issues.* That thought left me feeling hollow but also resolved that it was time for me to make a change."

■■■

Freedom comes by facing reality. Stepping away wasn't easy, but my father's realism helped him to leave his church gracefully. Today, the church he planted has become Hillsong Phoenix, under the capable leadership of Pastors Terry and Judith Crist.

Facing reality is powerful for those in exile. Jeremiah's writings pulsate with being realistic. Daniel's life is marked by sheer determination to call things as they are. Esther's mantra "If I must die, I must die" is yet another example. As exiles, our resilience depends on our becoming reality-recognition artists.

> Exiles are instrumental to God's purposes. During times of major change and intense pressure, exiles show the way forward. Exiles help to reform and revitalize the church, reorienting it toward God. A faith for exiles represents hope for the church.

In each of the previous chapters, we tried to look squarely at our present condition—specifically, how hard it is to make disciples in post-Christian digital Babylon. At the same time, we also wanted to remind our fellow believers, without equivocation, that the five practices we outlined lead to hope—hope that we find in Jesus. The church will find a way forward, even and especially in exile.

The first practice for resilient discipleship is *experiencing Jesus*, which relates to finding our soul's rest—our deepest identity—in Jesus. Problematically, churches often settle for presenting a cheap Brand Jesus imitation, just as our culture sells many false pretenses of identity. Clearing religious clutter to find closeness with and joy in Christ is the starting place for our discipleship efforts. Experiencing Jesus answers the deep longing of human hearts by answering the question *Who am I, really?*

The second practice is *cultural discernment*, which relates primarily to the life of the mind—how we think about and perceive our role in a post-Christian environment. Exercising wisdom is harder than ever because the increasing complexity of life correlates with the rising anxiety of our age. In response to these trends and in order to cultivate cultural discernment, churches must become robust learning communities that help people address deep questions related to *How should I live?*

The third practice is *meaningful, intergenerational relationships,* an objective of resilience that is often undone by powerful forces of isolation and mistrust. That is, society's centrifugal force of individualism tends to pull people apart, but the church puts people back together. We aspire to create a community in which people enjoy spending time together and want to emulate one another's lives. In so doing, we lay a foundation for one of the fundamental questions people ask: *Am I really known and loved by anyone?*

The fourth practice is *vocational discipleship,* which involves crafting integrated lives of purpose, especially in the arena of work. Teens and young adults today are smart, connected, ambitious, and career focused. The church can disciple them into their God-given callings—what they were made by their Creator to do—by reframing things such as ambition, generosity, productivity, and meaning. Vocational discipleship builds a foundation to help people wrestle to the ground questions such as *What am I called to do with my life?*

The fifth and final practice is *countercultural mission,* the relentless pursuit of faithful and fruitful presence in our communities by living differently from cultural norms (pursuing holiness) and trusting God to show up. Despite cultural pressures toward entitlement and self-centeredness, Christians pursue a life of sacrifice and service to others. But this isn't merely some social club for doing good; pursuing countercultural mission means acknowledging that God's design for life is much bigger than we can imagine and helps us address gnawing questions like *What is the significance of life?* and *What kind of legacy am I leaving?*

The promise of these five practices reveals the need for both realism and hope. For these five things to "work," we have to start with a realistic assessment of what makes them difficult to achieve.

Get Real

We have had so many conversations with pastors and teachers whose underlying (and sometimes overt) assumption is that what they do on weekends in worship services will be sufficient to bring about the kind of life change they hope to see in their people. David distinctly remembers having dinner with a good pastor friend who, upon hearing about the five practices we've covered in this book, said, "I think we've got those five things nailed with our new worship service."

What? Nailed? *I just told you about them*, David thought. *I must have described them inadequately, because it's almost impossible to nail these things.*

Pastors, you can't address the five resilient practices *only* in worship-service planning. And if you think you can, you're not being realistic. (Ask yourself if that is how you're operating. Most pastors have a hard time admitting how much of their time and attention are spent on weekend worship services.)

Parents, you cannot form your kids in the way of Christ just by taking them to church, even though this is very important.

Young Christians, if you want to be a resilient disciple, you've got to do more than attend worship. You have to engage in other spiritually formative practices.

If we want to follow Jesus with all our heart, mind, soul, and strength, all of us in modern exile must consider the total input and output of our faith. The input can't simply be a few hundred hours of passive church attendance a year.

While we're at it, let's talk about getting real in terms of the words we throw around as though everyone understands what we mean. From research we have conducted at Barna over the years, we know that many churches do not have consistent definitions for a disciple or even discipleship, among many other concepts.[1] And while most churches tell us that disciple making is one of the most important activities of the church, few pastors tell us they do it well.

If you'd like, please consider using the definition of discipleship we use in this book: to develop Jesus followers who are resiliently faithful in the face of cultural coercion and who live a vibrant life in the Spirit.

Part of getting real involves getting very specific. Defining terms. Clarifying goals. Keeping a hopeful vision at the center.

Resilient Hope

And finally we come to hope, which is among the most resilience-building gifts God gives. The research we've conducted for this study on the exemplary 10 percent of young Christians demonstrates that Jesus's work is alive and well among millions of young people today, just in the United States alone. This is not a fact to gloss over. As much as we might wring our hands in frustration, the gospel is burning bright in many, many young hearts.

More than mere concepts, these young disciples represent a hopeful future for the church. They embody the way of Jesus and show us how to follow him in digital Babylon.

Hope and realism. They go hand in hand.

You may remember reports of clergy abuse in Pennsylvania that emerged during the summer of 2018. More than one thousand victims came forward to testify to a grand jury about horrific experiences of sexual abuse by priests.[2]

Dr. Susan Reynolds recorded her experience at church on August 19, 2018, the Sunday *after* the shocking scope of the Pennsylvania crisis had hit the headlines. Her Twitter feed reflected how Mass unfolded that day.

> This morning at Mass, I witnessed something I have never seen, and words still mostly fail me. /1

> Our priest gave a powerful homily. He explained how poor ecclesiology has disempowered lay people &, in simple terms, how we must view this crisis as systemic. He affirmed the statement on the bishops' resignation. He concluded by calling for radical lay-led reform. /2

> Then he sat down. And then, in the fifth row, a dad stood up. "HOW?" he pleaded. "TELL US HOW." His voice was shaking and determined and terrified. His collared shirt was matted to his back with sweat. /3

> Jaws dropped. My eyes filled with tears. I've belonged to call-and-response parishes. This isn't one. This is a big, middle of the road parish in a wealthyish Southeast college town. In such contexts it's hard to imagine a more subversive act than doing what that dad just did. /4

> The priest stood up again. He looked the dad in the eyes, and he answered him slowly and haltingly and thoughtfully. The whole thing was so stunning I don't even remember what he said. But what he didn't say was, "Sir, please have a seat," or "We can talk after Mass." /5

He could have cited preservation of liturgical solemnity as an excuse to dismiss the man and thus escape this terribly uncomfortable moment. Instead, he let this father's cry interrupt us. He allowed himself to be put on the spot, to answer for things he didn't do. /6

"I have a son," the dad said. "He's going to make his first communion. What am I supposed to tell him?" In his searching, halting response, the priest made space for the wrenching inadequacy of every possible response to be laid bare. /7

This was not a brief, dismissive exchange. 10 minutes at least, and the two also talked at length after mass. At the end of mass, the priest offered to invite the Bishop to the parish for a listening session. "And if he won't come, I will." /8

The holy rawness of that dad's lament and the renegotiation of power it effected transformed the experience of the liturgy in ways that far exceed my ability to articulate them in this moment. /9

People don't want finessed press releases. They want to name their betrayal out loud, in public, in sacred space, before the tabernacle, before God and one another. They want to be listened to without condescension. They don't want easy answers. They want contrition. /10[9]

Dr. Reynolds's digital journal of events lets us feel the emotions in the church that day. Do you see the powerful interplay between realism and hope? There is confession, lament, and aching questions, which are all exercises in realism. But there is also hope, yearning for a better way. Can you imagine how much realistic hope people had to muster just to show up at church? Can you sense how connected that priest had to be to people's emotions and questions in order to pastor them? How much courageous anguish did the father have to find in himself to stand and publicly question the priest? There isn't a nice, tidy, gift-wrapped solution to sin and anguish. And yet the community of exiles finds a path forward.

Realism + hope = resilience

The circumstances described here may be extraordinary, but they represent the kind of emotion-laden experiences that are inevitable for all exiles. How clear-eyed can we be in our realism? How courageous can we be in our hope?

■ ■ ■

Here we are, at the end, and it feels like when I was taking my firstborn to Berkeley.

"I feel like there are a million things I'm forgetting to remind you."

There are so many things I'd still like to say, so many survey results I'd like to tease out, so many words from other wise people I'd like to leave you with. I would love to encourage you even more about the countercultural profile of young resilient Christians—all the ways we can have hope in what God is doing in them and through them.

You are living in the challenging age of digital Babylon, attempting to make (and to become) resilient disciples in a time when easy entertainment, comfort, and a kind of surface-level prosperity sing their siren song to lure us away from our truest selves and from the true God.

I am mostly realistic about what we are up against, and part of me even feels skeptical about the progress we can make, about the inexorable pull of digital Babylon. Digital Babylon presents us with challenges rarely experienced by the church. The allure of the screen age has surely undermined so much of what we as Jesus followers are trying to do.

And yet.

I am also bound to hope. Hopeful that young students like my daughter can enter the bastions of academia in our country and remain resilient disciples of Christ. Hopeful that the church, the bride of Christ, can become beautiful and transparent and true. Hopeful that, by cultivating these practices, we can form and be formed into disciples who thrive in digital Babylon.

Amen. Come, Lord Jesus.

Acknowledgments

Making books is a team sport. Our colleagues at Barna Group do awe-inspiring work, and we are honored to work alongside them. Savannah Kimberlin worked some stat magic in analyzing the data. Pam Jacob capably managed the entire project. Chaz Russo designed the cover and infographics. Many others supported the effort, including Brooke Hempell, Steve McBeth, Bill Denzel, Todd White, Brenda Usery, Jess Villa, Amy Brands, Roxanne Stone, Alyce Youngblood, Traci Hochmuth, Daniel Copeland, Gareth and Andi Russell, Rick Ifland, Brad Abare, Susan Mettes, and Brian Buffon. Welcome aboard, Mallory Holt and Aiden Dunn! We'll put you to work on the next one.

George and Nancy Barna: Thanks for creating an incredible company that continues to serve God's people.

Many reviewers made this better. Those who deserve special shout-outs include Nick Athens, Doug Colby, Lukas Naugle, and Scott Rae.

Aly Hawkins deserves heaps of praise and mounds of thanks for her remarkable efforts—yet again—to help turn our words and ideas into coherent words and ideas. You are a gift to us and to this book's readers.

Bill and Lorraine Frey: Your support for the Faith That Lasts project started this whole adventure. This book flows from your vision.

Baker Publishing is a flat-out awesome partner. Thanks to Dwight Baker, Mark Rice, Dave Lewis, Jack Kuhatschek, Rebekah Guzman, Kristin Kornoelje, and many others who work so hard on our behalf.

Thanks also to Jonathan Merritt and Chris Ferebee for their advice and input.

We want to thank our church communities: Reality (David) and Irving Bible Church (Mark). We have spent decades forming faith with parents, friends, children, teens, and adults. Certainly, this book reflects insights from our experiences together as imperfect people seeking to reflect Christ in the culture around us.

We are also so grateful to our families and especially to our parents: Gary and Marilyn Kinnaman, Tom and Judi Matlock, and Wayne and Kandy Lamb. Your support, not only for us but also for our children, is a gift.

From Mark

Dax and Skye Matlock: I love that you let me tell your stories even when doing it unfairly puts a magnifying glass on your own faith journeys. Never forget I love you.

David and Julie Grant, Shawn and Cheryl Small: Thank you for your friendship and transparency as we navigate grace, faith, ministry, and parenting together.

David and Stacie McDavid: Thanks for the endless conversations about culture, faith, and changing times.

Jade Matlock: This book has been deeply personal as we have reflected on research and our years of parenting. Thanks for being my best friend and partner for twenty-six years! You know how much I love you as we keep trying to figure out how to live for Christ and the kingdom in this crazy world. Here's to the empty nest!

From David

To the many, many dear friends who supported our family and prayed for us during the highs and especially the lows of 2017: Thank you! We could not have made it without you. Thanks especially to Eddie, LaDonna, Darcie, Aimee, and Cora.

Jill Kinnaman: Thanks for the bursts of laughter and the mountains of adventure. Life is sweet because of you. And thanks for the strength you display and the sacrifices you've made to allow Barna to grow and for this book to be crafted. You're an inspiration to me, and I love you.

Emily, Annika, and Zack: Being your dad is a greater joy than I could have possibly imagined. I am so proud of you for the people you are and the leaders you are becoming. This book represents my hope for your resilience, my prayer that you will love and follow Jesus into the very darkest of nights, and lessons we have learned together.

About the Research

Prodigals (ex-Christians): Individuals who do not currently identify as Christian despite having attended a Protestant or Catholic church or having considered themselves to be a Christian as a child or teen.

Nomads (lapsed Christians): People who identify as Christian but have not attended church during the past month. The vast majority of nomads haven't been involved with a church for six months or more.

Habitual churchgoers: Those who describe themselves as Christian and who have attended church at least once in the past month yet do not meet foundational core beliefs or behaviors associated with being an intentional, engaged disciple.

Resilient disciples: Christ followers who (1) attend church at least monthly and engage with their churches more than just attending worship services; (2) trust firmly in the authority of the Bible; (3) are committed to Jesus personally and affirm he was crucified and raised from the dead to conquer sin and death; and (4) express a desire to transform the broader society as an outcome of their faith.

Generations

A generation is an analytical tool for understanding culture and the people within it. It simply reflects the idea that people who are born during a certain period of time are influenced by a unique set of circumstances and global events, moral and social values, technologies, and cultural and behavioral norms. Barna Group uses the following generations:

Gen Z were born 1999 to 2015.
Millennials were born 1984 to 1998.
Gen X were born 1965 to 1983.
Boomers were born 1946 to 1964.
Elders were born prior to 1946.

Methodology

Throughout this book, you will read about research that is not directly footnoted. Those statistics and data-based statements have been derived from a series of national public opinion surveys sponsored by WisdomWorks and conducted by Barna Group between 2007 and 2018 for the Faith That Lasts project.

The main research examination for this book was conducted with eighteen- to twenty-nine-year-olds who grew up as Christians. This was a multiphase project that began with qualitative interviews.

All of the following studies are referenced in this book and were conducted by Barna Group among a national random

Date	Audience	Collection method	Sample size	Sampling error*
2009–2018	Barna's *Cities & States* database / US adults	Telephone and online	48,769	±0.5
February 16–28, 2018	US adults 18–29, current/former Christians	Online	1,514	±2.3
July 7–18, 2017	US teens 13–18	Online	507	±4.2
November 16, 2016, to January 17, 2017	US Protestant youth pastors	Online	335	±5.3
January 2–10, 2016	US adults 18–30	Online	803	±3.3
November 4–16, 2016	US teens 13–18	Online	1,490	±2.3
November 8–16, 2016	US engaged Christian parents of teens	Online	403	±4.8
November 4–16, 2016	US adults	Online	1,517	±2.3
January 8–20 and February 3–11, 2015	US adults	Telephone and online	2,010	±2.0
April 29–May 1, 2015	US adults	Online	1,025	±2.9
June 27–28, 2015	US adults	Telephone	1,012	±2.9
July 3–9, 2015	US adults	Online	1,237	±2.6
August 17–21, 2015	US adults	Online	1,000	±3.0
August 24–26, 2015	US adults	Online	1,000	±3.0
July 2014	Christian clergy	Telephone and online	1,449 (1,286 Protestant; 163 Catholic)	±2.4
July 2014	Clergy from other faith traditions	Telephone and online	159	±7.7
August 18–22, 2014	US adults 18–30	Online	1,000	±3.0
October 10–15, 2013	US adults 18–29	Online	843	±3.2
December 2012	US adults	Telephone	1,008	±2.9
January 2011	US adults 18–29, current/former Christians	Online	1,296	±2.7
January 2011	US adults	Telephone	520	±4.3
December 2010	US adults 18–29, current/former Christians	Online (pretest)	150	±8.0
August–December 2009	US adults 18–35	Telephone	20	Qualitative

*Percentage points; sampling error reflects a 95 percent confidence level.

sample of the population identified. Upon completion of each survey, minimal statistical weights were applied to the data to allow the results to more closely correspond to known national demographic averages for several variables. All the surveys among adults included a subsample of people drawn from cell phone households. All studies relied on callbacks to households not reached after the first attempt; a maximum of six callbacks were made to each nonresponsive household, with contact attempts made at different times of the day and days of the week. The average length of the surveys in these studies ranged from fifteen to twenty-two minutes.

When researchers describe the accuracy of survey results, the estimated amount of sampling error is often provided. This refers to the degree of inaccuracy that might be attributable to interviewing a group of people that is not completely representative of the population from which the people were drawn. The maximum amount of sampling error is listed in the table. That estimate is dependent on two factors: (1) the sample size and (2) the degree to which the result being examined is close to 50 percent or the extremes, 0 percent and 100 percent. Keep in mind that there is a range of other errors that may influence survey results (e.g., biased question wording, question sequencing, inaccurate recording of the responses provided, inaccurate data tabulation, etc.)—errors whose influence cannot be statistically estimated.

Notes

1. Dr. Martin Luther King Jr., from a sermon delivered at Temple Israel of Hollywood, February 26, 1965, accessed November 2018, https://www.americanrhetoric.com/speeches/mlktempleisraelhollywood.htm.

2. Andy Crouch and Barna Group teamed up to create *The Tech-Wise Family* (Grand Rapids: Baker Books, 2017), which helpfully addresses many of the challenges of raising children in the digital era.

3. Thanks to Chad Ragsdale of Ozark Christian College for his thoughtful input on the Jerusalem versus Babylon motif.

4. We recognize there are many ways to define culture and that, in some sense, there is no such thing as a singular culture.

5. Pastor Roger Valci at Valley Christian Center in Dublin, California, eloquently expresses these ideas.

6. Jean Twenge, "Have Smartphones Destroyed a Generation?" *Atlantic*, September 2017, accessed April 2018, https://www.theatlantic.com/magazine/archive/2017/09/has-the-smartphone-destroyed-a-generation/534198/.

7. Richard Freed, "The Tech Industry's Psychological War on Kids," Medium, March 11, 2018, accessed July 2018, https://medium.com/@richardnfreed/the-tech-industrys-psychological-war-on-kids-c452870464ce.

8. There are many estimates of screen and media use, including some that are even larger than those we describe here. We have used some of our own from Barna as well as drawing heavily on the following secondary

research: "Generation M²: Media in the Lives of Eight- to Eighteen-Year-Olds," Henry J. Kaiser Family Foundation, January 2010, accessed July 2018, https://kaiserfamilyfoundation.files.wordpress.com/2013/04/8010.pdf.

9. Barna Group, *Spiritual Conversations in the Digital Age: How Christians' Approach to Sharing Their Faith Has Changed in 25 Years* (Ventura, CA: Barna Group, 2018), 39.

Practice 1 To Form a Resilient Identity, Experience Intimacy with Jesus

1. You might wonder at prodigals' apparent inconsistencies. Why would respondents sometimes call themselves Christian but at other times reject that term? At Barna, we often find that people answer religious questions in unpredictable ways. Looking beneath the numbers, we have personally run across many young ex-Christians who haven't had the courage to admit to others their dwindling faith status. A good friend of David's, who is in his twenties, a guy raised in the faith from birth, recently texted that he is no longer a Christ follower, but he hasn't told his parents yet. "I'm not against any of it. I just don't follow anymore." In some ways, it actually takes a lot of courage for prodigals to admit to *themselves* where they have landed spiritually.

2. Credit to my friend Greg Thompson, who I have heard describe "elective identity."

3. Barna Group, *Gen Z: The Culture, Beliefs and Motivations Shaping the Next Generation* (Ventura, CA: Barna Group, 2018).

4. Barna Group, *The State of Discipleship* (Ventura, CA: Barna, 2016).

Practice 2 In a Complex and Anxious Age, Develop the Muscles of Cultural Discernment

1. Henry A. Kissinger, "How the Enlightenment Ends," *Atlantic*, June 2018, accessed May 2018, https://www.theatlantic.com/magazine/archive/2018/06/henry-kissinger-ai-could-mean-the-end-of-human-history/559124/.

2. Tara Haelle, "Hospitals See Growing Numbers of Kids and Teens at Risk for Suicide," NPR, May 16, 2018, accessed May 2018, https://www.npr.org/sections/health-shots/2018/05/16/611407972/hospitals-see-growing-numbers-of-kids-and-teens-at-risk-for-suicide.

3. Barna Group, *The Porn Phenomenon: The Impact of Pornography in the Digital Age* (Plano, TX: Josh McDowell Ministry, 2016), 66.

4. Noah Kulwin, "One Has This Feeling of Having Contributed to Something That's Gone Very Wrong," *New York Magazine Select All*, April 17, 2018, accessed April 2018, https://nymag.com/selectall/2018/04/jaron-lanier-interview-on-what-went-wrong-with-the-internet.html.

5. For instance, 1 Timothy 1:19 says that if a person deliberately violates their conscience, their faith can be "shipwrecked"—vivid imagery for the care our faith requires.

Practice 3 When Isolation and Mistrust Are the Norms, Forge Meaningful, Intergenerational Relationships

1. Barna Group, *The State of Pastors: How Today's Leaders Are Navigating Life and Leadership in an Age of Complexity* (Ventura, CA: Barna, 2017).

2. We have seen this quote attributed to Stanley Hauerwas, but we've heard Twitter can be unreliable.

3. Thanks to Eugene Peterson for this phrase, which comes from his book *Leap Over a Wall: Earthy Spirituality for Everyday Christians* (San Francisco: HarperOne, 1998).

4. These concepts are developed in Bonhoeffer's *Life Together* (New York: Harper & Row, 1954), which my father, Gary Kinnaman, helpfully recommended during a time of my own disillusionment with church.

5. The "Theology of the Body" is St. John Paul II's integrated vision of the human person. See John Paul II, "The Theology of the Body," 2016, accessed August 2018, www.theologyofthebody.net.

6. Barna, *The State of Discipleship*, 46–47.

7. "What Is the Church?" from Covenant Membership, the Village Church, 14, accessed November 2018, https://thevillagechurch.net/Content /ExternalSite/Documents/Covenant%20Membership%20Class/Campus %20SF%20Pastor%20-%202018%20-%20Covenant%20Membership%20 -%20Membership%20Covenant%20-%20Revised%20-%20Book%20-%20 Web%20-%20Covanant%20membership%20section%20only.pdf.

8. Barna, *The State of Pastors*.

9. Richard Ross, Twitter post on July 22, 2018.

10. Check out Pete Scazerro for information about emotionally healthy churches and emotionally healthy leaders. www.emotionallyhealthy.org.

11. Richard Beck, "A Peculiar People: Emotions and Spiritual Formation," *Experimental Theology*, May 17, 2018. http://experimentaltheology .blogspot.com/2018/05/a-peculiar-people-emotions-and.html (accessed February 2019).

12. Stephen Marche, "Is Facebook Making Us Lonely?" *The Atlantic*, May 2012. https://www.theatlantic.com/magazine/archive/2012/05/is-facebook -making-us-lonely/308930/ (accessed February 2019).

13. Marche, "Is Facebook Making Us Lonely?"

14. Andy Crouch, *The Tech-Wise Family: Everyday Steps for Putting Technology in Its Proper Place* (Grand Rapids: Baker Books, 2017).

15. John Rampton, "8 Reasons Why Happy Couples Rarely Share Their Relationship Statuses on Social Media," *Inc.*, May 1, 2017, https://www .inc.com/john-rampton/8-reasons-why-happy-couples-rarely-share-their -relationship-statuses-on-social-m.html (accessed February 2019).

Practice 4 To Ground and Motivate an Ambitious Generation, Train for Vocational Discipleship

1. Keaton and his family have allowed us to share this story publicly. It also appears in Bob Goff, *Multi-Careering* (Grand Rapids: Zondervan, 2014). Keaton is a published author!

2. "Teenagers Want Successful Careers and Global Travel, Expect to Delay Marriage and Parenting," Barna, May 10, 2010, accessed August 2018, https:// www.barna.com/research/teenagers-want-successful-careers-and-global -travel-expect-to-delay-marriage-parenting/.

3. We discovered this insight in our work with the Association of Biblical Higher Education, and the findings are included in two reports: *What's Next for Biblical Higher Education* (Barna, 2017) and *What's Next for Christian Higher Education* (Barna, 2018).

4. *The Empire Strikes Back*, directed by Irvin Kershner (San Francisco: Lucasfilm Ltd., 1980).

5. Benjamin Franklin, *Poor Richard's Almanack*, December 1743.

Practice 5 Curb Entitlement and Self-Centered Tendencies by Engaging in Countercultural Mission

1. David Kinnaman, *Good Faith* (Grand Rapids: Baker, 2016).

2. James Davison Hunter, *To Change the World* (Oxford: Oxford University Press, 2010).

3. Jean Twenge and W. Keith Campbell, *The Narcissism Epidemic: Living in the Age of Entitlement* (New York: Atria Books, 2009).

4. See research on parents' desire for safety in Barna's report called *The State of Youth Ministry* (2016), which we conducted in partnership with Youth Specialties and YouthWorks.

5. See Barna's report called *Making Space for Millennials* (2015).

What's Next: Finding Hope in Exiles

1. Consider checking out Jonathan Merritt's excellent book in which he addresses the challenge of the fading efficacy of religious terminology and language. *Learning to Speak God from Scratch: Why Sacred Words Are Vanishing—and How We Can Revive Them* (New York: Convergent Books, 2018).

2. While the story specifically involved the Catholic Church, it represents the kind of crisis that any faith community can and does face. For example, 2018 saw prominent stories about public moral failure in Protestant churches as well; the point is to consider the impact of something so horrible as clergy abuse and how that affects living faithfully in exile.

3. Susan Reynolds, Twitter post from August 19, 2018.

David Kinnaman is the coauthor of *unChristian, You Lost Me*, and *Good Faith*. He is the president of Barna Group, a leading research and communications company that works with churches, nonprofits, and businesses ranging from film studios to financial services. Since 1995, David has directed interviews with more than one million individuals and overseen hundreds of US and global research studies. He serves on the board of Biola University in southern California, where he lives with his wife and their three children.

Mark Matlock has been working with youth pastors, students, and parents for more than two decades. He is the principal at WisdomWorks, a consulting group dedicated to helping churches and faith-centered organizations leverage the transforming power of wisdom to accomplish their mission. Mark is the former executive director for Youth Specialties (YS) and creator of the PlanetWisdom teen discipleship conferences. He has written more than twenty books for teens and parents. In addition, Mark is an ordained minister serving as a member of Irving Bible Church and serves on several boards including the American Bible Society. Mark and his wife live in Texas and have two adult children.

E-Courses Designed to Help You Put the Research into Action

Are you preparing young disciples for a world that no longer exists?

Bring the insights from *Faith for Exiles* to your home or church with two practical e-courses taught by David Kinnaman and Mark Matlock.

Raising Resilient Disciples for Parents provides detailed training on the five practices described in this book, prompts three essential conversations about the research, and shows clear steps to take together as a household.

Building Resilient Disciples for Church Leaders gives pastors and church teams detailed training on the five practices from David Kinnaman, as well as facilitation training sessions with Mark Matlock. This e-course also includes an assessment process to measure and identify opportunities for growth in your church and hands-on tools to help you accelerate the implementation of your findings.

These in-depth e-courses provide you with practical ideas and encouragement to rethink discipleship—making resilience a priority for life in digital Babylon.

Barna   Start your e-course at
faithforexiles.com or **barna.com/faithforexiles**

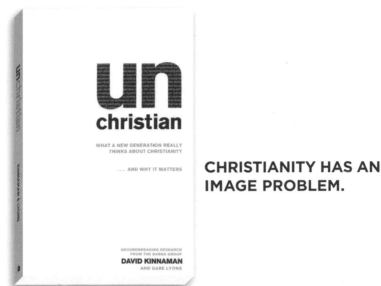

CHRISTIANITY HAS AN IMAGE PROBLEM.

UNCHRISTIAN:

WHAT A NEW GENERATION
REALLY THINKS ABOUT CHRISTIANITY . . .
AND WHY IT MATTERS

BY DAVID KINNAMAN AND GABE LYONS

The book that captured a generation's perceptions of Christianity continues to stir conversation about the gap between the way Christians are perceived and the way they actually desire to live.

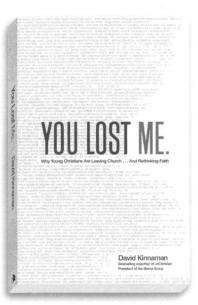

DAVID KINNAMAN HELPS YOU FIND FAITH WITH A NEW GENERATION.

YOU LOST ME:

WHY YOUNG CHRISTIANS ARE LEAVING CHURCH . . . AND RETHINKING FAITH

"In this insightful and engaging work, Kinnaman, president of the Barna Group, presents findings from interviews with young adults, aged 18 through 29, who have left Christianity. Kinnaman investigates what young adults say about their religiosity or lack of it, in order to help churches retain young adult membership. Kinnaman's research is thorough and his results are fascinating. . . . [His] practical problem-solving approach, along with his repeated assertion that 'every story matters' . . . make the work a must-read for anyone concerned about the future of Christianity."

—*Publishers Weekly* starred review

LIKE THIS
BOOK?
Consider sharing it with others!

- Share or mention the book on your social media platforms. Use the hashtag **#faithforexiles**.

- Write a book review on your blog or on a retailer site.

- Pick up a copy for friends, family, or anyone who you think would enjoy and be challenged by its message!

- Share this message on Twitter, Facebook, or Instagram: I loved #faithforexiles by @BarnaGroup // @ReadBakerBooks.

- Recommend this book for your church, workplace, book club, or class.

- Follow Baker Books on social media and tell us what you like.

 ReadBakerBooks

 ReadBakerBooks

 ReadBakerBooks